S0-AXV-019

THE PARABLES OF THE LORD

THE PARABLES OF THE LORD

RICHARD GUTZWILLER S. J.

HERDER AND HERDER

1964

HERDER AND HERDER NEW YORK
232 Madison Avenue, New York 16, New York

Translated from *Die Gleichnisse des Herrn*
(Einsiedeln: Benziger Verlag) by Arlene Swidler.

Nihil obstat: Patrick A. Barry
Censor Librorum

Imprimatur: ✠Robert F. Joyce
Bishop of Burlington
March 23, 1964

The parables reprinted herein are taken from *The New Testament,* translated by James A. Kleist S.J. and Joseph L. Lilly C.M. Reprinted with the permission of The Bruce Publishing Company, Milwaukee. Library of Congress Catalog Card Number: 64-19729
© 1964 by Herder and Herder, Incorporated
Printed in the United States of America

Contents

Fulfillment of the Kingdom of God

Foreword

THE parables of our Lord attract and fascinate his followers in every generation. Others, it is true, such as Socrates and Aristotle, Cicero and Quintilian, also made use of parables. But the parables of Jesus stand alone. A. T. Cadoux has remarked that whereas in other forms of art, such as drama or epic and lyric poetry, a smaller cluster of great souls stands together on the highest peak of achievement, no one in the art of parables stands near Jesus.[1] Since so much of our Lord's teaching is enshrined in parables (Mk 4:33–34), a few general remarks about the nature of parables will not be out of place here.

At its simplest, the parable has been defined as "a metaphor or simile drawn from nature or common life, arresting the hearer by its vividness or strangeness, and leaving the mind in sufficient doubt about its precise application to tease it into active thought."[2] We are all fond of similes (which liken or compare one thing with another) and metaphors (which identify one thing with another or predicate of one thing the qualities of another). We easily remember examples of these figures of speech from the Gospels: "Woe to you, scribes and Pharisees, hypocrites! because you are like whited sepulchres" (Mt 23:27). "I am the light of the world" (Jn 8:12).

The simple metaphor may be expanded into a more elaborate similitude or full-length story by the addition of details.[3] For a more elaborate similitude, consider Mt 7:3–5: "But why dost thou see the speck in thy brother's eye, and yet dost not consider the beam in thy own eye? Or how canst thou say to thy brother, 'Let me cast out the speck from thy eye'; and behold, there is a beam in thy own eye? Thou hypocrite, first cast out the beam

[1] A. T. Cadoux, *The Parables of Jesus*, New York 1931, 11
[2] C. H. Dodd, *The Parables of the Kingdom*, New York 1961, 5
[3] Ibid., 6. A simile, of course can be expanded in like manner.

7

from thy own eye, and then thou wilt see clearly to cast out the speck from thy brother's eye."

The Germans call this more elaborate similitude *Gleichnis,* a word which appears in the original title of this book. They reserve the term *Parabel* for that metaphor or simile which has been expanded into a story by the addition of details calculated to develop a situation or capture the imagination. Though the story may vary in length from very short to full scale, this is what we commonly call a parable proper. It is admitted on all sides that a clear line of distinction cannot be easily drawn between simple figurative sayings, elaborate similitudes and parables proper.[4]

It is not difficult to distinguish parables from fables, wherein we have a developed simile with a story founded upon some imaginative and usually impossible situation, as when "trees went to anoint a king over them" in Judges 9:8. However, it is much more important to carefully distinguish parable from allegory, which is a developed metaphor, or perhaps better, a story comprised of a series of details each of which is a separate metaphor with an assigned significance of its own. The parable, on the other hand, usually has but one lesson derived from one single point of comparison. In a parable, the various persons, places, or situations have no independent figurative signification in the story. As one writer has put it: once the central point of the parable has been discovered, the remaining details may be discarded as "trimmings." This is the theory of the matter. But in practice this distinction between parable and allegory must not be urged too absolutely. In the first century A.D. Quintilian, the head of a Roman school of rhetoric, recognized that often alle-

[4] Ibid., 7

8

gorical details with a significance of their own are to be found in a true parable.

Modern biblical scholarship has produced many fine studies on the parables of Jesus from a critical viewpoint.[5] Virtually all authorities on the subject insist on a sharp distinction between parable and allegory. Following Adolph Jülicher, who exercised strong influence on subsequent writers, most biblical scholars attribute to the early Church the creation of any allegorical elements found in the Gospels. More recently, the whole question has come up for reexamination.[6] In many quarters, Jülicher's total rejection of allegory is now acknowledged to be an oversimplification. Certain details in the Gospel parables simply demand an exposition of their own proper signification. The studies of Fiebig[7] and Hermaniuk[8] reveal that it is no longer possible to hold for Jülicher's sharp distinction between parable and allegory, if the Semitic mentality be rightly considered. A study of ancient Hebrew writings, both sacred and profane, indicates that the Hebrew term *mashal* (pl. *m^eshalim*) includes the notions not only of parable and allegory but also of many other literary forms, such as proverbs, maxims, fables, and the like. Father Raymond Brown observes[9] "there is no reason to believe that Jesus of Nazareth in his *m^eshalim* ever made a distinction be-

[5] Besides the works of Cadoux and Dodd, the following should be noted: A. Jülicher, *Die Gleichnisreden Jesu*, Freidburg-i-B: 1898–1899, 2 Vols.; B. T. D. Smith, *The Parables of the Synoptic Gospels*, Cambridge 1937; J. Jeremias, *The Parables of Jesus*, tr. from the sixth German edition 1962, New York 1963.

[6] Cf. the significant article by Raymond E. Brown, "Parable and Allegory Reconsidered," *Novum Testamentum* V, Leiden 1962, 36–45. Father Brown has also written in popular style a worthwhile pamphlet, *The Parables of the Gospels*, Glen Rock, N.J. 1963.

[7] P. Fiebig, *Altjüdische Gleichnisse und Gleichnisse Jesu*, Tubingen 1904, and *Rabbinische Gleichnisse*, Leipzig 1929.

[8] M. Hermaniuk, *La Parabole Évangélique*, Louvain 1947.

[9] "Parable And Allegory Reconsidered," 38

tween parable and allegory. He was a popular teacher and would naturally favor simple stories, so we need not look for the complicated allegories that the Fathers found. But simple allegory, and metaphors already familiar to his hearers from the OT— these lay within his illustrative range." To attribute all identifications proposed in the Gospel to explain allegorical elements in the parables to a spontaneous introduction by the primitive Church fails to consider the distinct possibility that Jesus himself may have offered the original identifications.[10]

Modern biblical scholarship has focused attention on other interesting problems concerning the parables.[11] For example, different Gospels place the same parable in different settings (Cp. The Parable of the Marriage Feast in Mt 22:1–10 and in Lk 14:15–24). Again, different Gospels present the same parable to different hearers (Cp. The Parable of the Lost Sheep in Lk 15:3–7 and in Mt 18:12–14). Finally, the same parable sometimes has different meanings in different Gospels, often according to the different audiences and situations (Cp. The Parable of the Lamp in Mk 4:21, in Mt 5:14–16, and in Lk 11:33). What was the original setting and signification of these and other parables in the ministry of Jesus? Frankly, we cannot always tell.[12] Many of the parables seem to have been directed to our Lord's enemies, especially to the Pharisees.

As transmitted to us in the Gospels, the parables often reveal to us a situation proper to the early Church rather than the actual situation of Jesus when he taught in parables. Rudolf Schnackenburg remarks: "This actual situation of Jesus can be

[10] Ibid., 45

[11] For the whole problem of the parables, cf. J. Jeremias, *op. cit.*, 11–114.

[12] As Father Brown observes, it is better to admit that at times we simply do not know the original setting of a parable than to force the parables into an exegetical strait jacket by arbitrary reconstructions. Cf. *The Parables of the Gospels*, 18

10

most important in an interpretation of the parable but frequently it is overshadowed and obscured by the actual situation of the early Church which applied the parable to its own situation and possibly understood it differently. We can detect traces for instance not only of moralizing tendencies but also of the altered historical position after Easter, the missionary situation and the postponement of the Parousia."[13]

As we turn from this brief sketch of the more important aspects of the modern historical approach to the study of the parables, we may be tempted to wonder if they have anything more than historical value for us today. It is comforting to know that critical scholars themselves are aware of the same temptation. At the conclusion of his study of the parables, C. H. Dodd remarks[14] that the parables are works of art, and any serious work of art has significance beyond its original occasion. "Their teaching may be fruitfully applied and re-applied to all sorts of new situations which were never contemplated at the time when they were spoken. But a just understanding of their original import in relation to a particular situation in the past will put us on right lines in applying them to our own new situations." The present work proposes to apply the teaching of the parables to the daily life of every Christian. Composed originally to be preached, these moving spiritual conferences reveal the penetrating mind and intense apostolic zeal of a priestly soul pleading with all of us to live a more fruitful life in Christ. The author's conception of a true Christian faithful to his baptismal calling is an inspiring one. That he has meditated long and prayerfully on both the parables and contemporary Christian life is immediately evident.

Father Gutzwiller views all creation as a parable bearing a

[13] R. Schnackenburg, *God's Rule And Kingdom*, New York 1963, 144
[14] *Op. cit.*, 157

11

meaning beyond itself. Sin has made it difficult to look upon this world as the sign of another. Unlike the parable which reveals, the world distorted by sin disguises. Jesus, the great teacher in parables, came to show us how to look correctly again upon the world. "He reads the book of creation and understands the speech of creatures. Everything speaks to him of God and the kingdom of God. . . . The colorful fullness of reality, the abundance of nature and of life, all begin to speak, to sound, to ring out. All become the visible word through which the invisible God speaks to men. The invisible is made visible and inaudible audible. The incomparable makes itself known in the parable."

In the ringing, eloquent tones of the orator, Father Gutzwiller applies the teaching of the various parables to problems which concern the faithful christian living in today's world. In a literary style calculated to move the heart as well as to challenge the mind to decision, he presents each study with clarity, precision and definition. Like all Gaul, this book is divided into three parts: The Divine in the Kingdom of God, The Human in the Kingdom of God, and The Fulfillment of the Kingdom of God. Into this framework, the author fits his study of the various parables. In each study the reader is brought face to face with one or another of the basic responsibilities of true Christian living in the modern world. The author raises most of the questions troubling many sincere Christians of our times. His balanced answers reflect his awareness of the present need to change some things as well as his deep respect and reverence for what is of permanent value from the past. No serious Christian can fail to profit from a prayerful reading of this challenging application of the parables to contemporary spiritual problems.

Providence College   THOMAS AQUINAS COLLINS O.P.

Parables: Sense and Meaning

GOD is the incomparable. Every attempt at comparison shows once again that God is the completely other, the in-every-respect greater, absolute majesty. Because everything created is limited and incomplete, from it we learn first of all what God is *not*. This negative theology is of great importance, for it makes any humanization or secularization of God impossible.

And yet there stand in the bible these words of God: "Let us create man after our image and likeness." What man of himself would scarcely have dared he now may and must attempt on the basis of these words of God: he can see the created as a likeness of the creator. For creator and creature have one thing in common: being. Both are distinguished from nothing, and thus being makes possible a comparison. But then it is immediately clear that being, though common, is at the same time in its innermost essence basically different. For God is of himself and in himself. Creation is of God and through God. Thus creation bears a meaning beyond itself and shows that a comparison may never become an equation, but only a parable. This means that in all diversity a mutuality can be found in a third, a tertium comparationis. Thus man can recognize from creation not only what God is not but also what God is.

Sin however has seized destructively upon this possibility of parable. It has dimmed the view of men so that they see and yet do not see. And it has done this in two ways.

13

First, man's view goes astray in creation. This world is to him no longer a sign of another but is in itself the ultimate and supreme. He makes the world his god. But because there is only one God this world he adores becomes an idol, a counterfeit god. Instead of leading man to God in the character of a parable the world seduces him into his own ego; it disguises rather than reveals. Man in this world is then no longer a copy of God, but wishes to be the original. The satanic "You will be as God" is not an allusion to parable, but to equality.

Sin has made the parable character impossible in a second way, for it has distorted the world and man. The savage and ugly, the violent and unbridled, the unrestrained, the chaotic has broken into creation. Therefore man, when he contemplates the world, will err about God. Sometimes the world seems so beautiful to him that he imagines he finds something divine in it and deifies it. Then again it seems so ugly to him that he does not recognize it as the work of God and denies God. Pantheism and atheism are opposed to the parable character of creation.

But Jesus came and taught us again to see the world correctly. As the son of God he knows God as no one else can. And as the son of man he knows about the world and human life as no one else can. Thus he can vault the daring arc between the two shores as the great pontifex, as the bridge builder between God and man. He sees the world again as a likeness of God. In him as logos shines the image of the father, and in his pure humanity shines the ideal of Adam: imago Dei. Speaking in parables is actually Jesus' typical manner of proclaiming the message of God. In the gospels there are more than seventy parables of the lord, while there are scarcely any in all the other writings of the new testament. Miracles and parables are the signs which Jesus gives, the miracles as a supernatural sign of divine intervention and the parables as a natural sign of creation. Jesus need not search for parables. They surround him on all sides. He creates out of the fullness of being. He reads the book of creation and understands the speech of the creatures. Everything speaks to him of God and the kingdom of God: the birds of the air and the flowers of the field, the rushing water and the pale lightning, the ripening grapes and the stray sheep, the woman who kneads the dough and the thief in the night, kings and slaves, children and beggars, soldiers, whores, farmers, priests, shepherds and tradesmen. The colorful fullness of reality, the abundance of nature and of life, all begin to speak, to sound, to ring out. All become the visible word through which the invisible God speaks to men. The invisible is made visible and the inaudible audible. The incomparable makes itself known in the parable.

If men now still see and yet do not see, hear and yet do not hear, then they are at fault. For then their eyes are not blind but dazzled, their ears not deaf but closed. It is the hardening of Pharaoh which says no in every age. But whoever wishes to see and hear can understand anew the meaning of creation. All that is bright, beautiful, majestic, grand is a sign of the unending bright light, of a boundless beauty, of an indescribable majesty, of an all surpassing grandeur. The finite becomes a parable of infinity, a signal fire of eternity, a guidepost to God. And everything dark, hard, bitter, ugly becomes a likeness of the defection from God and of the fall into the underworld and the subhuman, a parable of the kingdom of darkness of satan and all demons. Between these two worlds man is situated, the world of God above him and the world of satan beneath him. Parable extends

15

beyond passive, innocuous contemplation; it is a challenge to man, a summons to take sides and make decisions.

Thus the parables have their own beauty and attraction, so that the people say of the lord: "He speaks as one who has power." They can understand him, follow his words, truly feel the seriousness and force of his words. On the other hand the parables contain something disturbing for men, for they are riddles and reflections of reality. They show man that he sees only in speculo et aenigmate (1 Cor 13), and waken the longing to see face to face, so that the disciples can say joyfully: "Now you speak openly and no longer in parables" (Jn 16:29).

The old teachers of Israel have written that the law of Moses is a heavy basket, a seething hot cauldron, but one without handles. In the parables of Solomon one finds these handles; the parables of Christ the lord do more. They have not only given us the handles to the law, but hold out to us the sweet fruit which lies in the basket and the fragrant wine in the heavy pitcher—the wine that makes the wise eloquent and lovers intoxicated. Ask the saints! Learn from the mystics! He who understands the parables of the lord is led by Christ out of the world to God, guided through all parables to the incomparable.

The Divine in the Kingdom of God

The Newness of the Kingdom of God

NEW WINE

Mk 2:22: "No one pours new wine into old wine skins; otherwise the wine will burst the skins, and the wine is lost as well as the skins. No; new wine belongs in fresh skins."

Christianity was something new, no longer the outward observance of the law but inner grace; no longer a chosen people but a message to all mankind; no longer fear but love; no longer the awaiting of a future messias but God in our midst. This coming of God, this forceful breakthrough of the divine into the human, of eternity into time, was something so violent, so vast that it could not merely be added like a patch to an old garment. It burst all existing forms; it was fermenting, foaming wine which one did not dare to pour into old, brittle skins. It was a new beginning of world history, a morning sparkling, a spring bursting forth. It was truly the year 1.

Thus it was once. But is it still? Is christianity today still fermenting new wine? Has it not long since been reduced to a harmless, sweet tasting sodawater of middle class respectability? Is it not an insipid sugarwater of a cheap hope in the next world, as we live in the midst of this world which we cannot remake? Is it not numbered in the 2414 canons of the

Codex Juris Canonici? Is its prayer not hardened in the strict formulas of the breviary, the litanies, the rosary? Is its enthusiastic worship not inexorably regulated through the rubrics of the liturgy? Are the foaming waters of its faith not constrained in the iron pipes of scholastic concepts and dogmatic syntheses? Has the vitality of the mystical body of Christ not become a withered skeleton of organization? Has the mighty stride of its conquering courage not been degraded to the defensive warfare of fruitless foxhole apologetics? Has the roaring lion, as he still stands before us in the gospel of Mark, not long since become a docile housepet whose occasional growling is swiftly appeased by stroking him soothingly with a concordat or with monetary advances? Are the blazing fires of its love, which loosed the chains for the slaves and kissed the lepers, still burning in our charitable organizations and institutions? Are not the intellectual wings of its eagles so clipped through censorship, indexes and imprimaturs that they are no longer able to dwell on the mountains of spiritual daring?

New wine? Once upon a time . . .

Again and again, secretly or openly, these reproaches are raised against us. Alongside the bolshevik storm christianity is only quiet, tired murmuring. Beside the young swelling strength of new ideas, mounting movements and revolutionary might christianity has the kindly but tired, withered countenance of a venerable old woman.

Is the reproach justified? There are two things which must be examined. First, christianity as vitality in *individuals*. Here it is something constantly new. In every man it is a new beginning, a new birth. It comes in baptism as strength into the soul of man become christian, to transform him into the image of

18

Christ: imago Dei. In him it must truly be like fermenting new wine. In him it must be living breath, revolutionary strength, always shaping and transforming his life anew. But this wine of christian faith may not be poured into the old, brittle skins of an ordinary, purely natural human life. This means that man may not be first of all a purely natural man like others and then, in addition, a christian besides. Rather he must in his practical life be a christian first of all and form his entire human conduct from there out. He is not primarily a physician, lawyer, merchant or housewife and then a christian besides, but he is first of all a christian and determines and forms his vocation from this fact; the christlike physician, the christlike businessman, the christlike wife are therefore different from others. He is not first of all a German, a Frenchman, an Italian, a Swiss, and then a christian besides, but he is first of all a christian and then determines his relation to the state, to the nation, to the race. If the opposite were true then christianity would be just mere patches on a garment, new wine in old skins. In every prayer, in every reception of the sacraments this fermenting, foaming wine fills again the human chalice, the tempest of the spirit of God blows again through all the corners of the soul, the stream of life circles from God again through men. So christianity in individuals is something eternally young, eternally new. Where it is not, piety is not completely genuine.

But christianity as a vital force in *humanity?*

Is it not paralyzed in form and tradition? Christianity *must* have forms. They are in part founded by Christ himself, in part built up by men. Thus both divine and human are comprised in the forms of christianity. Christ established a visible church. He himself determined its organizational structure in the peo-

19

ple, the apostles and Peter, in the faithful, bishops and pope. He instituted sacraments: baptism with water, the eucharist with bread and wine, penance with the judgment upon those whose sins are forgiven or whose sins are retained, and so on. Christ himself used a formula for prayer. He prayed the traditional psalms and taught us the Our Father. Forms therefore are an expression of his will; they must exist. Centuries have labored on their development. In the *liturgical forms* of our worship we trace the sound of hebrew in "hosanna," "alleluia," and in God "sabbaoth;" we hear the greek tones in the "kyrie eleison," and perceive the latin-roman propriety in the language of the mass and in the entire construction of our liturgy. The breath of the same spirit which animated the primitive church in Jerusalem, the pauline community in Greece and the christians in Rome perceivably permeates the liturgical mass celebration of every catholic church and chapel. In the dogmatic *formula of our credo* the annual rings of the mighty tree of the catholic church can be unmistakably counted. Our fathers chiseled at this formula at Nicea and Ephesus. And thus we know: it is the same faith then as today, the same Christ yesterday, today and for eternity. The venerable *formulas of our prayers* span thousands of years. These psalms were prayed by the shepherd lad David and sung by the christians with subdued voices in the catacombs. This same Te Deum was celebrated by the church in the radiant morning of freedom following the centuries of persecution and was rung by the ecclesia militans after a thousand spiritual battles and a thousand and one victories. There is something great in a tradition that produces its structure and its character in a permanent form. Does not everyone feel the difference between praying in a modern concrete church and in the half dark of a venerable cathedral? It is one thing to go into one of our new suburban churches and another to celebrate the mass perhaps in the cathedral of Chur, in the great cathedral at Cologne or in the Basilica of St Peter in Rome. There one feels the movement of the passing centuries. In these holy places christendom of past days has cried and prayed, implored and sung. Tradition is something great. It is the root foundation which gives stability and permanence. It is the arch of the bridge which binds together the past, present and future.

So we rejoice reverently in the forms which a two thousand year tradition has created and do not wish to dispense with it. But we may not make absolute the time-conditioned within it; we may not deify the human, not exchange the unimportant and accidental for the necessary and essential. Papal authority remains even when there is no longer a church state. The spirit of religious orders and vows remains even when the tonsure is no longer clipped and the habit no longer worn. The ardor in the heart of the savior of the world remains even when we sing other sacred heart hymns. And not every society which has statutes and an executive board is guaranteed eternal permanence. Permanent forms can also conceal the danger of torpidity. When the spirit no longer animates, the body becomes a cadaver and the form a skeleton. In a tightly joined, venerable old house the spider webs can fill the corners, the dirt can heap up, the musty air can suffocate if the windows are not ever anew thrown open that the storm of the Spirit can enter in, if all the rooms and corners are not gone over again and again with the broom of reform. And the most beautiful chalice will be soiled and stained if it is not purified again and again that it may be a vessel worthy to bear the blood of Christ. Whenever the skins

21

become fragile we throw them away, not to pour the wine of christianity on the ground, but into new skins, into usable forms.

Christianity is born of God, is the divine in humanity, and is therefore never old. Always new, always fermenting, foaming, fiery wine. We must carry it in the skins of stable forms. Formless christianity is impossible. Unchristian forms are useless. What is needed is a vital christianity in large, God-given, tradition-proved forms or in new forms created out of spiritual necessity. Formlessness and the destruction of all tradition is barbaric and unchristian. To encrust and suffocate with empty forms and traditions is senile and likewise unchristian. Vital worship in venerable, great forms, old and new, is in the christian spirit. Thus where forms really are outmoded, really are brittle, discard them calmly. But above all take care that your christian faith really is fiery wine; then you will feel for yourself which skins are brittle and which are still good. The spirit decides.

The Kingdom of God as a Free Gift

THE LABORERS IN THE VINEYARD

Mt 20:1–16: "The kingdom of heaven reminds me of a landowner who went out at break of day to hire laborers for his vineyard. After agreeing with the laborers on one denarius a day, he sent them into his vineyard. Again he went out about nine in the morning and saw others loitering about the market place. 'You men, too,' he said to them—'go into my vineyard, and I will give you whatever is right.' So they went. Again he went out about noon and three in the afternoon, and acted in the same way. Finally, going out at five o'clock, he found still others loitering about, and said to them: 'Why have you been loitering here all day?' 'Because,' they replied, 'no one has hired us.' 'Well, then,' he went on to say, 'you too—go into my vineyard.' When evening came, the owner of the vineyard said to the overseer: 'Call the laborers together and pay them their wages; begin with the last group and end with the first.' Then the five o'clock group came forward, and everyone received one denarius. Now, when the first group came, they supposed they would receive more; but they, too, received one denarius each. They accepted it, but grumbled against the landowner. 'These late arrivals,' they said, 'have done but one hour's work; yet you put them on the same level with us who have borne the whole day's burden and scorching heat.' 'But, my friend,' he argued with one of them, 'I am doing you no wrong. Did you not agree with me on one denarius? Take what is yours and make off; but I choose to give this last arrival as much as I gave you. Have I not a right to do as I please with what is my own? Or, do you take it amiss because I am generous?' Just so will the last be first, and the first will be last."

There is something provoking about the parable of the workers in the vineyard. It invites contradiction. To begin with, the picture itself is impossible. What vineyard owner would have no notion of how many workers he needed to bring in the grapes on the day of harvest! After hiring his force in the morning he must make his way from the vineyard to the city gate four more times to hire still more laborers. Still more impossible is his method of paying; he gives directions to begin with the last and to let those who came first, who are tired and exhausted, wait the longest. And most impossible of all is his schedule of wages. He gives all the same amount, without any regard for work time and work load. The protest of the injured is understandable and appears justified. Our sympathy is involuntarily on their side. Otherwise what is the meaning of social justice!

Accordingly the application of the picture to the reality of the kingdom of God seems just as impossible. Apparently there is no proportion between burden and wages. Why exert oneself? Why bother? Is it not better to belong to those who are called late, who take life easy on the broad and comfortable highway and only at the end take the turn into the steep and narrow way to heaven, there to find the same happiness as the others who strive for decades to fulfill the divine will in selfless sacrifice and renunciation? Somehow this attitude undermines noble impulses.

Christ consciously and deliberately gave his parable this challenging formulation in order to show that we do not approach the real essence of God and our relation to him with our everyday concepts and ideas from human life. God is the completely other. He is sovereign freedom. God is the lord who can decree and decide according to his own discretion, his own judgment and option. "May I not do what I wish with my own?" The image of the potter who molds the soft clay into any form he chooses is repeated frequently by the prophets and is drawn with uncomfortable sharpness by Paul in the epistle to the Romans. Against God there are no rights and no claims. All belongs to God. Every fulfillment of his desire, every work commissioned by him, every completion of his demand is a self-evident claim which he as creator raises and which man as created must comply with. Of earnings and payments, in the strict sense, there can be absolutely no question. When Christ nevertheless uses this word in the gospel it is only in a transferred, essentially weakened sense. The pharisee who appeals to works and results, who derives a claim from them and who, as it were, submits the account to the lord is shown by Christ to be a religious impossibility, a caricature of the interior attitude. The relationship between God and man is not to be grasped with bourgeois-democratic concepts. Rather the complete sovereign freedom and free sovereignty of God as absolute lord must be unconditionally recognized. God decrees in full freedom whom he calls, which men and which peoples. And he decrees in this same sovereign freedom when this call will go forth to men and to peoples. It is not the man or the people who choose God; men and peoples are chosen by God. The call is a grace which goes forth at the time, to the place, to the men and to the group which God as the freely choosing has ordained. The primacy of grace is the basis of the christian spirit.

And only now comes the second consideration, one which gives the parable a happy turn. God uses his freedom not for calculating and careful weighing but for abundant blessing and pardoning. He dispenses with full hands even where there is no claim, and not in an extended or weakened sense. In his epistle to the Romans Paul recalls the example of Esau and Jacob, the one chosen already in his mother's womb, the other rejected in his mother's womb. But the rejection of Esau is only provisional. For after the defection of Jacob Esau was also to be blessed and pardoned, and in the end the rest of the descendents of Jacob would again return home to the lord. If God leaves all to the disobedient, it is only that in the end he may pity all (Rom 11:32). Human pettiness, with its calculating pedantic spirit, does not wish to understand the freedom of God. But the lord answers: "Are you jealous because I am generous?" The mystery of predestination resolves itself in the end in the incomprehensible mystery of grace, a grace which all, when in the next world they finally gaze upon it clearly, will recognize with amazement and wonder as the heaped up, overflowing

25

abundance of God. Then each of us will see that the call which came forth to him, the moment which was chosen for this call, the power to answer this call and cooperate with it, the constant guidance and support, and the final election is the incomprehensible, unearned grace of the lord. Those called late will perceive with astonishment how much richer before God were the lives of those called early. But they will not be envious. And those called early will perceive with equal amazement that the lord in the abundance of his love also pardons munificently those called late. But they too will not be envious. And both together will perceive and acknowledge with amazement that almighty God in his goodness reckons the smallest actions of man, the unreflected and taken for granted ones, as worthy of merit, and names eternal life his reward. Thus, finally, all will lose themselves in astonishment at God's grace.

What to the trivial, calculating spirit of man seems senseless and unjust proves itself in the greatness of the spirit of God a dissolution of the limits of mere justice through the greater power of the giving love. God shows his freedom and sovereignty in the grace which he gives. Here is the real meaning of this apparently meaningless parable. Man must feel the provocation of the parable; then it will be a summons to him to go forth out of the narrowness of his thinking in order to stride into the spaciousness of the spiritual world of God.

Growth of the Kingdom of God

THE GROWING SEED

Mk 4:26–29: "What happens in the kingdom of God is something similar to what takes place when a man has sown the seed in his field: he sleeps at night and awakes in the morning; meanwhile the seed is sprouting and shoots the stem into the air—he himself does not know how. For of itself the earth bears fruit, first blade, then ear, then ripe grain in the ear; and when the crop permits, he at once applies the sickle, for the time for harvesting has come."

The word automatic is dangerous for the religious life. It awakens the image of a soulless mechanism or a comfortable passivity. And yet it appears here in the gospel, and indeed as the word of the lord. He compares the growth of the kingdom of God with the growth of the seed and stresses that the earth "of itself"—in the greek text "automatically"—brings forth fruit. The growth of the kingdom of God is likewise "of itself."

The thought surprises us at first. We are accustomed to judge the harvest as the yield of human work. But if the situation is considered more exactly man is seen to take care only of peripheral details. Over the existence of the fruit he has no power at all. He can drain the earth, plow it up, fertilize and nourish it; he can promote the growth through watering and irrigating; he can protect the plants from damage. But growth is that which we call the mystery of life, the inner capability of development which lies in the seed, the peculiar dynamic of the living. Out of this its indwelling strength the seed grows—spontane-

27

ously, automatically. This strength the parable of Jesus stresses expressly, for it says that this growth goes on unceasingly. The plant pushes through the surface of the ground, grows to a stalk and ripe ears, unconcerned whether man is sleeping or awake, whether it is day or night. The growth proceeds constantly.

Just so, according to the word of Jesus, is the kingdom of God. Here too man can do a number of things, but here too it is only the peripheral. He can prepare himself for the reception of grace; he can clear away the impediments; he can follow and collaborate with grace. But grace as such is precisely grace, something whose nature does not lie within the scope of man but is essentially supernatural. But here in this word of Christ is a forceful recognition that this grace is something living, something which unfolds, develops and grows. Grace means not merely that God looks at man differently than before and is thereby more gracious to him; grace is also a new existence which is placed within man, a new life which is given him. For this reason Christ speaks also of the rebirth, that is, of the gift of a second, new life. Grace grows like all living things. Its beginning is not the doing of man but the act of God, not human activity but the vitality of grace. It guards itself against all cramped asceticism and all attempts to force the religious life in order to extort its results. The farmer who arises in the morning has no fear that he has lost time through his sleep, for he knows that his seed has also grown during the night. So also the religious man must not live in perpetual anxiety that he is not doing his work, that he has passed up opportunities, that grace languishes in him. He lives in quiet confidence that God works in him by day and by night, and that as a result the kingdom of God grows in him from day to day.

The same holds true for the kingdom of God in the world. The church is a supernatural life principle of human community, a seed God has laid in the field of this earth which has come up and now continues to grow, ripening constantly until the harvest of the last day. The kingdom of God grows in the light days of the peaceful times of church history, in the years of man's enthusiasm and peoples' joyful readiness. But it also grows in the dark nights of persecution, of opposition and of bloody suppression. It grows because it has within itself the living strength to grow which no man has given it and no man can take away. Here too men can through their activity accelerate the growth. But the decision lies not in their hands but in the strength of the kingdom of God itself. Here too this recognition guards against a false activism, stormy jingoism, nervous haste and anxious last minute panic. It grows through the strength of God. And it grows from day to day, through all steps and stages until the grain fields of the lord are ripe for cutting. In the Apocalypse the impatient question of how long God will wait before intervening is answered with the reply that the number of the chosen must first be filled. In other words, despite bloody persecutions the number of the called and chosen constantly grows and, as a result, the harvest of the kingdom of God constantly multiplies and betters itself. In the midst of the coming and going of dynasties, in the blossoming and withering of cultures, in times of economic advancement or depression, in the discussions of the decline or renewal of the west, in the catastrophes of past or threatening world wars the kingdom of God grows constantly and incessantly out of its own interminable vital energy. The knowledge of this automatic growth gives the believing examiner of world and human history a rare calm and superiority, for it shows him that a vital energy is active in world events, an energy which is in its innermost being and growth independent of human experience and plans and of all destructive forces, because it is divine.

Thus there lies in the parable a calming, happy optimism. It has nothing to do with mechanism, for life is no wound-up machine. The danger of passivity is avoided, for the farmer has his full measure of work to accomplish, but he knows that the decisive factor lies not in this work but in the vital energy of the seed. So too in the religious life man has his own work to do, but in the knowledge that the decisive factor lies with God, and that this factor is grace. Human acts are only an acting with. Human progress is only a progressing with. The real acting, working and progressing is accomplished by God. God and man therefore work together, but God primarily and God decisively. He gives the grace which dwells within the vital energy. In this sense grace acts automatically. For God himself is that "strength that works, moves, and creates all."

THE MUSTARD SEED

Mt 13:31-32: "The kingdom of heaven reminds me of a mustard seed which a man carefully plants in his field. This is the tiniest of all seeds; but the full-grown plant is larger than any garden herb and, in fact, becomes a tree, so that the birds of the air come and settle in its branches."

The parable of the mustard seed tells us that where God is at work the greatest grows out of the smallest. The mustard seed is so small that it can scarcely be seen on the palm of the hand. But when laid in the earth it grows so quickly and so forcefully that it becomes the largest shrub in the garden, and even the birds can sit on its branches. God needs no great beginning and no apparatus. Most of God's works begin small and obscurely, unpretentiously and without noise. But because they are the works of God they develop without interruption and display in just this apparent disproportion between beginning and completion the working of the hand of God.

So it was with the words of Christ. Plain and simple is their sound, and huge is their working. Christ says to Peter: "You are the rock and on this rock I will build my church." And from the words that were spoken in remote Caesarea Philippi to a galilean fisherman have come the greatness of the papacy, pilgrimages from the whole world to the grave under Michelangelo's dome, and the recognition of the roman primate by all bishops of the globe. Christ says to the small group of eleven in the evening hour of the last supper: "Do this in my memory." And from the mustard seed of this word comes the splendid blossoming bush of the modern mass liturgy, so rich in meaning in all its solemn splendor. Christ says to the few men gathered round him: "Go into the whole world." And the bubbling spring of this word grows to the mighty, broad stream of the christian mission movement flowing into all continents. Christ says: "What you do for the least of my brethren you have done for me." And the simple word releases the social and charitable exertions of all centuries and generations, continually providing impetus for new blossoms of corporal, spiritual, financial and

31

moral works of assistance. Christ says: "If you desire to be perfect, go and sell all that you have and follow me." And the few words become the great response of complete dedication to the following of Christ in the marital, religious and single states. They fall like a little mustard seed into the hearts of thousands of young people and grow into the blossoming garden of true Christian aspiration.

The same holds true for the kingdom of God as a whole. It began as a mustard seed, small and unpretentious, with a few plain men and women in a despised province of the roman empire. But it has grown to a world church which more than five hundred million people joyfully profess and whose authority and moral significance constantly grows. Again and again have the branches from these mustard shrubs been torn away, and attempts made to root out the seed. But this seed has ever again begun to sprout and the roots bud, and the new twigs have become greater and stronger than the old. Succisa virescit! Humiliations have exalted the church. Persecutions have confirmed her. Defeats have become victories. The hand of God has laid the mustard seed in the very soil of this earth.

The same holds true of the *movements* within this church, for example the religious orders. The hours of grace of the quiet monks of Subiaco grow into the majestic, forceful work of the Benedictine world. The young beggar of Assisi renews the whole church through the Franciscans. And out of the vigil in which a knight of Manresa consecrates doublet and dagger to the mother of God in order to become a knight of Christ, there grows the Jesuit order and its fight for God's honor.

The same holds true of the amazing work of many other saints. Out of the unknown shepherd maiden of Lorraine comes

32

Joan of Arc as the leader of the french army. And the weakest seminarian becomes, as curé of Ars, a renewer of the clergy. The unknown nun in the Carmel at Lisieux becomes the celebrated favorite of the catholic world.

The same holds true for the religious inner life of a christian. It begins invisibly and unpretentiously in baptism. The mustard seed is laid there in the earth of the soul. Then it grows in the course of the christian life—invisibly of course, but for all that amazingly. And only in the next world will we see, astonished and admiring, that the tiny beginning has released tremendous growth and that the christian life produces an inner development whose size and beauty we with our eyes bound to earthly things cannot imagine.

Thus again and again can the same law of growth be recognized: out of the smallest comes the greatest, for the great God is not bound to earthly size.

Whoever compares the magnificently developed mustard shrub with the little mustard seed must praise God.

Fruitfulness of the Kingdom of God

OF THE VINE AND THE BRANCHES

Jn 15:1-8: "I am the real vine, and my Father is the vinedresser. He prunes away any branch of mine that bears no fruit, and cleans any branch that does bear fruit, that it may bear yet more abundant fruit. By now you are clean, thanks to the lessons I have given you. Remain united with me, and I will remain united with you. A branch can bear no fruit of itself, that is, when it is not united with the vine; no more can you, if you do not remain united with me. I am the vine, you are the branches. One bears abundant fruit only when he and I are mutually united; severed from me, you can do

33

nothing. If one does not remain united with me, he is simply thrown away like a branch, and dried up. Such branches are gathered and thrown into the fire to be burned. As long as you remain united with me, and my teachings remain your rule of life, you may ask for anything you wish, and you shall have it. This is what glorifies my Father—your bearing abundant fruit and thus proving yourselves my disciples."

Attachment to the church is not merely something external, purely legal or only moral, as is perhaps the attachment through a similar conviction of faith or through the uniting bond of love; rather it is something substantial and vital. Christ calls himself the vine and his disciples the branches. Yes, it is true; all natural life is ultimately a sign and a metaphor of supernatural life. The attachment to Christ through grace is more intimate, stronger and more alive than the natural attachment of the branches to the vine. And therein lies the secret of the fruitfulness of human life.

Without the attachment to Christ life is unfruitful. "Without me you can do nothing," says the word of the lord clearly and unyieldingly. To someone outside, a life may seem to be crowned with success. It may exhibit creative works of art, profitable results and political gains and awake the amazement of the world and posterity. Nevertheless it is before God unfruitful and dead if it was not lived in Christ. Even religious works, for example practices of piety, penance and pastoral work, are blighted with unfruitfulness if they are not done in Christ. For "only one is good, God." And therefore only what is done in God, or more precisely in the God-man Jesus Christ, is good.

External activism in churchly life has meaning and worth then only if it flows from the attachment to Christ.

With Christ life is fruitful. It may outwardly seem completely insignificant and worthless. It can be the unnoticed performance of a day laborer, the infirmity of someone incurably sick, the failure of one shattered by life, and can nevertheless be fruitful before God if the work, the sorrow and the sacrifice is done in Christ. Being and acting in Christ is the secret of fruitfulness. Thus alongside the substantial attachment to Christ through grace there is also need for a conscious attachment in thought, desire and love of man, an attachment which is furthered through prayer. Ora et labora, prayer and work essentially belong together. For the men who work in the kingdom of God prayer is no loss of time, for it is a filling up of the reservoirs which feed the work, the collecting of potential energy which can be turned into kinetic. The christian works out of another world into this world. Therefore he must keep the contact with that other world constantly alive. Whether the worlds are joined by being alongside one another, "contemplata tradere," or whether they are merged in one another, "in omnibus quaerere Deum," is a difference of ways and means, of psychological temperament, of type, but one thing is common to both: the work springs from the attachment to Christ. Only thus is pastoral care fruitful. All preaching and teaching, helping and organizing, in short every kind of work for the kingdom of God, must have its nourishment therefrom. Whoever does not live in attachment to Christ will sink into the world. Then the branch of the vine is torn away and condemned to unfruitfulness.

Young people dream of future successes, men and women in the high noon of life test the strength of their efforts, and people in their autumn ask themselves apprehensively what has come out of their lives. The answer lies in the word of Christ: "Whoever remains in me brings forth much fruit." Not visible success, not the opinion of men, not even one's own evaluation determines the worth or worthlessness of actions, but living in Christ. Vinery that is torn away from the vine is good for nothing, not for building, not for cutting, not for furniture, but only for burning. Just this wood, usable for nothing else, bears the sweetest fruit of the wine. Apparently useless men become through their attachment to Christ bearers of bursting berries and shoots. And apparently efficient men are without Christ only the kindling wood of God. Existence in Christ is in the full sense of the word decisive.

THE GRAIN OF WHEAT

Jn 12:24–25: "I tell you the plain truth: unless the grain of wheat fall into the earth and die, it remains just one grain; but once it has died, it bears abundant fruit. He who holds his life dear destroys it; he who sets no store by his life in this world will preserve it for eternal life."

One could easily deceive himself on what it means to live in Christ and imagine that christianity simply brings something new to natural being, that it is only, as it were, an extension of nature. In that case revelation would be merely a reaffirmation of the view that christian morals are nothing else than a deepening of that which man already naturally recognizes as good. To be a christian would be nothing but an enlargement of the natural personality, its faculties and talents, the final product an artistic production of psychology. And the christian would be the perfect harmonious man.

But this is not the case. To be sure, Christ used images from organic life. But in order to circumvent every illusion he pointed out that the growth of the organism and the mystery of its fruitfulness presume something completely other, namely death itself. If the grain of wheat does not die it brings forth no fruit. Fruitfulness in Christ is, so to speak, beyond the natural-organic and yields its harvest only out of the grave of the old man. A fruitfulness of religious life which does not proceed from a death of the ego is illusion. Grace is a new creation and an awakening from the dead (Rom 4:17). The suppression of self proceeds from this. It is therefore not merely further development and unfolding to completion; it is something completely other, coming from without and from above, not growing from beneath and within. The supernatural is not simply a further development of the natural.

Accordingly revelation is also the conveyor of new perceptions, but perceptions which the human spirit does not understand even after the reception of revelation. The sacrificium intellectus as a part of this struggle is essential for faith. Christian morality is not simply refined humanity, it is an excessive demand by God. "Be perfect as your Father in heaven!" Christian sacraments are not mere symbolism of human completion; the demise of the old man and the creation of the new in baptism introduces us to a completely other world, inaccessible to the natural man.

And with this thought in mind it will be completely clear how cruelly serious Christ meant this death; he used this simile of the grain of wheat in connection with his own death on the cross. The parable is concerned therefore with not merely natural death but also unnatural violent death. The catholic ascetic with its demand of mortification has its source here. The cross does not stand somewhere on the edge of christianity but in the center. The connection of the branches with the vine is a connection of christians with the crucified lord. Jesus therefore enjoins: "He who holds his life dear destroys it; he who sets no store by his life in this world will preserve it for eternal life." He speaks not of the natural development of the ego and its gifts of the spirit and the heart but of the losing of the self, yea even the hate of self. Only suppression leads to salvation. And therefore christianity is not an affair of pedagogy and psychology but of asceticism, not an affair of self-development but of self-denial. The parables of the wood of the vine and the wood of the cross belong together. Through these it is shown that it is indeed organic growth out of which true fruitfulness springs—not however the growth of a natural organism with the natural laws of growth and fruitbearing, but of the mystical corpus Christi with the law of the cross and the secret of death as strength for life and fruitfulness.

The truth of the story of the grain of wheat can be seen in the christian attitude toward life and in the history of the church of Christ. And this story will find its final fulfillment when the grain of wheat of the earth dies at the end of the world and the new earth as a new creation of God brings the realization of all the dreams of paradise. Then will the words of the Apocalypse that the tree of life bears fruit in all twelve months hold true. For then earthly life will be changed through death into the new life of immortality. "See, I make all things new."

The Dynamics of the Kingdom of God

LEAVEN

Mt 13:33: "The kingdom of heaven reminds me of a handful of leaven which a housewife mixes with three measures of flour, to work there till the whole mass has risen."

Two extremes must be avoided: the secularization and the desecularization of christianity.

Through the incarnation of God christianity belongs in the world. Every desecularization, no matter how much it is pursued under the appearance of the good, is a contradiction of the God-become-man and thus a contradiction of the essence of christianity. But the danger of secularization also lies herein. In Christ this danger is eliminated by the divinity of his person. In christians on the other hand only too human traits are entwined with the human, thereby requiring the false strands to be unraveled again and again.

History and the present offer rich material for the contemplation of secularization as well as of desecularization.

Secularization has repeatedly shown itself through an involvement in alliances with kings, parties and armies and the consequent sharing of their fates; through the amalgamation of throne and altar; through a false confidence in power, diplomatic relations and high-level protection. Secularization is also displayed in a too easy relinquishing of certain social strata, the nobility or middle class, the bourgeoisie or the workers. Liberal catholicism and conservative catholicism are both dangerous in their one-sidedness. There is also secularization in the intellectual life through a too rigid adherence to a false astronomical, geocentric world picture, false biological opinions, false interpretations of the age of the earth and man and the like. The nationalism of christian missionaries, the intrusion of bourgeois ideals into the christian way of life, rationalism in theology, the canonization of certain directions in art are all mere entanglements with the world which harm christianity.

But desecularization is also a danger, and today it is the greater. Christianity and the world lie too far from one another.

False ideas and theories play a role in the writings of some christian authors—perhaps an exaggerated eschatologism, a onesided liturgicism or a false mystique of the merely contemplative. To these erroneous theories there is added a spiritually false belief in the flight from the world merely to preserve the white cloak of Cassian unspotted, whereas actually the soiled mantle of Nicholas finds a better reception at the gate of heaven. Or a false fear of the world because it is supposed that the world really belongs to the devil. Or an unchristian contempt of the world which rejects everything "mundane" as only vanity of vanities.

But on the part of the world also false theories are apparent. A false interpretation of culture and progress which pays attention only to the externals of technical development, of material well being and of external civilization. A false concept of humanism and humanity which makes man the center and the measure of all things. A false understanding of the deciding factors of the historical development in marxism. A false theory of national sovereignty which proclaims the state alone competent to determine right. And alongside these false ideas are false attitudes, such as the fear of the might of the church or an elusive hope for an earthly paradise.

So church and state, religion and culture, christianity and the world are completely separated far from one another, to the detriment of both.

Here the parable of the leaven has something to say. The leaven tightly shut up in the kitchen cupboard is worthless. And the measure of flour in the bowl is just as worthless. Only when the two are combined, when the leaven is in the measure of flour, does good bread result. So also must christianity be the ferment of the world. This is precisely what Pius XII expressed with the formula: "The church is the life principle of human society!" It is what the soul is to the body, the animating, informing strength.

The church as a whole must stand in the midst of the neopagan world in order to work on it, shaping and forming it. There is no locking oneself in a catholic ghetto, no retreating into catholic towers. Christ sends the lambs among the wolves, the minority into the midst of the overwhelming heathen majority, relying upon the strength of the Holy Ghost. Thus the dialog with modern philosophy, cooperation in the solution of social problems, assistance in the building of a new community of nations, the introduction of christian ideas, forces and personalities into films, into the theater, are all necessities. Certainly christianity is not of this world, rather it is in the midst of it, and indeed not as a completely foreign substance but as the strength which brings home a secularized or undivinized world to God and, through union with God, gives back to the world its own innermost essence.

The parable however is also valid within the church. We have for years and decades spoken of the formation of an elite and the training of cadres in the catholic camp. We have sought out the best in all levels of the population in order to train and form them in professional groups, training courses, study weeks, retreats, marian congregations, societies and vacation camps. We have also worked with the masses through demonstrations, general conference meetings, congresses, through mass organizations and newspapers and magazines designed for the masses. But we have not yet brought the two elements together correctly and entirely. The leaven is too little in the flour. The elite segregates itself; the mass is left alone. With inbreeding and self-sufficiency, with ghetto mentality and airs of superiority, with esoteric little groups of selected spirituality the parable of the leaven cannot be realized. An officers' corps without army, captains without ships are as ineffective as the army without leadership and an entire fleet without a sense of direction. Only where the elite stands within the mass, forming it, is the parable of the lord realized.

We must be serious about the parable of the leaven, theoretically through a correct teaching of the relation of nature and supernature, practically in the correct grasp of a consciousness of mission, a right method of the apostolate. When the pope calls the laity and creates specifically lay organizations, when priests again seek contact with the proletarian population, it is a good sign that clergy and laity are striving in common to enter into the modern world as the leaven of Christ in the flour.

Not a secularized or desecularized christianity, and not a heathen world, but only a christianized world can give hope for a better future.

The Value of the Kingdom of God

THE TREASURE IN THE FIELD

Mt 13:44: "The kingdom of heaven reminds me of a treasure buried in the field: as soon as a person discovers it, he hides it again, and off he goes in his joy and sells all his possessions and buys that field."

This time the little ox tugged powerfully, almost mischievously. The peasant therefore drove his plowshare more deeply than usual into the earth and turned over furrow after furrow, until the work was suddenly interrupted by a harsh metallic noise. Involuntarily the animal stopped. The man lifted the primitive plow aside, dug up the earth with his hands and found to his boundless surprise a large heavy earthen pot which was filled to the rim with coins and expensive jewels—shining pieces of silver and glittering gold. How intoxicatedly he burrowed there awhile, letting the coins slip through his fingers, wondering at the rare earrings and precious bracelets. Then he looked around very carefully to see whether anyone had observed him, heaped the earth over it again, plowed a shallow furrow over the surface to conceal his discovery, laid an especially large stone there as a marker and plowed the little field to the end. One single thought filled him now, so filled him that he could no longer work peacefully by day or sleep by night! This field must become his property. As long as he was only an employed day laborer it was impossible for him to appropriate the buried treasure. But where could he get the money to buy the field? At last he sold his entire possessions. He sold his hut and the few chickens and

43

sheep which he owned. He borrowed still more from friends and acquaintances until he had enough ready money together that he could pay the owner a fancy price for the field. His wife was inconsolable. His sons reproached him. His neighbors shook their heads. He seemed to them no longer right in his wits. But he was indifferent to all this protestation for only he knew his secret. Finally the field was his own and with it the buried treasure within, which apparently had been brought there for security before the last war and whose owner had not survived. With it his price was returned a hundredfold; he would pay all his debts and build a larger house; he was a man whose fortune was made, envied by his enemies, congratulated by his friends, secure for his entire life.

Christ compares the finding of the kingdom of heaven with the finding of such a treasure. The worth of the kingdom of heaven is so great that every sacrifice and every effort repays itself. To one who has grasped what the kingdom of heaven is all else is secondary. Only this one thought can fulfill and animate him. All lines must meet at this one point for him, all efforts must be directed to this one goal, his entire life must be filled with this one secret: the reality of the kingdom of God. The kingdom of God has the character of eternity, while all else passes. It makes man a son of God, a brother of Christ; it gives him citizenship in the kingdom of the father in heaven.

It provides him with completely new prospects which are otherwise closed even to the greatest scholars and brightest men. It gives him new strength through which all his actions are lifted to a higher level and through which alone they become meaningful before God. It gives him a final inner security which bars all anxiety. It puts his relation to other men in a completely new light. In one phrase: he is lifted into a new super-earthly life and his entire earthly life is changed. Nothing can be compared to the kingdom of God. Its worth goes beyond all worth. All measurement fails in this infinity. All scales quickly tip. All calculation collapses. For the kingdom of God is divine and hence the breaking of the divine existence into the human, the encompassing and fulfilling of human existence by the completely other, the divine. Is any effort too great in seeking this kingdom? Is any venture too daring? Any sacrifice too painful?

A superficial christianity is then no longer possible. One can no longer perform a fleeting morning or evening prayer and completely lose sight of the kingdom of God for the rest of the day. It is no longer possible to attend a silent mass on Sunday for the kingdom of God and tolerantly sit through a sermon so that one may feel free to pay no more heed to the kingdom of God for the rest of the week. It is unthinkable therefore to be completely absorbed in one's profession merely to earn money or in expectation of the evening relaxation and enjoyable weekends, and to attend to the kingdom of God only at the end of life. Superficial christianity has never comprehended what christianity really means. The real christian has a secret that those standing outside do not understand. Martyrs have given their lives for it. Thousands have their possessions and goods confiscated, sacrifice their homelands and families, careers, positions, good names, all for the sake of the kingdom of God. Others may shake their heads at this thought, criticize it, express doubts, raise objections. They do not know the secret. The precious treasure is hidden from their eyes. They see only the earth and know not what it conceals. Only the visible externals, the materials of life, are for them real. The background, the divine aspect of the kingdom of God is to them an unknown quantity. The christian knows what life means. The others do not know. Therefore the christian's conviction, his inner attitude, his judgment is completely different. He is the misunderstood, for many the incomprehensible. And yet it is he alone who has rightly comprehended what life really is. And it is he who in the end will be envied and congratulated. He who has understood gives up all, as the gospel says, joyfully. The superficial christian sacrifices unwillingly. The real christian sacrifices gladly because he knows why. He knows that the greatest effort is still too small.

Through the incarnation of God in Jesus Christ the kingdom of God was buried in the field of this world and time as a precious treasure. There are too few who find it and draw out of the discovery the consequences.

THE PRECIOUS PEARL

Mt 13:45–46: "Again, the kingdom of heaven reminds me of a merchant in quest of beautiful pearls: as soon as he discovers one pearl of great value, off he goes and promptly sells all his possessions and buys it."

There are men who find religion a burden, the law of God a yoke under which they must bow, and the church a wall which narrows their freedom. They perceive that all these things must exist because God has so decreed, and they resign themselves in the consciousness of the power and dominion of God. Of the glad tidings there is not a trace; there is only religiosity as a duty.

Much different is the parable of the precious pearl. According to it the kingdom of God is something so rich, beautiful and radiant that man gives up all else joyfully in order to win this one thing.

The kingdom of God is something eternal. Everything else is bound and fixed by time, delivered up to corruption and marked with death, and therefore in the end worth nothing at all.

And the kingdom of God is blessedness, happiness, joy, jubilation. Therefore the images of a jewel, of a wedding feast, of the blooming bush. Moreover man is created for joy. So that if a joy without end beckons to him, everything will be so overshadowed by this light and splendor that beside it nothing else prevails.

What does the loss of fortune matter if it wins for us the kingdom of God! What does the sacrifice of life matter if it is exchanged for eternal life! Cheap painted fragments of glass alongside the precious pearl! Crumpling pretensions yield to the infinity of God and the true human greatness that comes through God. Fading beauty is severed from the imperishable beauty of the transfigured body and of the heart flooded by the love of God.

Religion therefore is not a duty but a privilege. The law of God therefore is only a yoke if man is not filled with the interior freedom of the children of God. The church is confining only for him who absolutely insists on going into error. But to whomever lives in God religion is joy and freedom.

Of course only faith can open the eyes of man to this vision. He who has never seen the splendor of the high mountain ranges will feel more at ease in the wooden hut of the dark valley. He who has never traveled on the high sea will lead an apparently content existence in the little pond, until one day he sees the magnitude and beauty of the mountains and the sea and recognizes immediately that he himself has barricaded the entrance. He who has once seen the precious pearl is no longer left in peace. This unrest is a special grace. Only when man no longer sees christianity as a hard "Thou shalt," as a memorized catechism formula, as moralizing chicanery, as a mortgage taken over from his forbears, but rather as a call to the heights, as a step into freedom, as marriage with God will the religious conviction palpable in the gospels again live and give christendom its world conquering, violently engagé, transforming and unconquerable strength. We must once again let the precious pearl flash and shine in her gleaming beauty. A christianity that has nothing scintillating about it has not understood the parable of the precious pearl.

The Human in the Kingdom of God

Asking

THE PARABLE OF THE IMPORTUNATE FRIEND

Lk 11:5–13: "Suppose some one of you has a friend and goes to him at midnight and says to him: 'Friend, lend me three loaves of bread; a friend of mine has just turned in from the road to visit me and I do not have a thing to set before him': shall then the man inside remonstrate and say: 'Do not pester me; at this late hour the door is barred; my little ones are in bed with me; I cannot get up and accommodate you'? I tell you, he may not get up and accommodate him just because he is his friend, but he will certainly get up for shame's sake and give him all he asks for.

"That is what I say to you: ask, and you will receive; seek, and you will find; knock, and you will gain admission. In fact, only he who asks receives; only he who seeks finds; only he who knocks will gain admission.

"Again, suppose some one of you, fathers, is asked by his son for a loaf of bread: will he hand him a stone? Or, when he asks for a fish, will he hand him a serpent instead of a fish? Or, when he asks for an egg, will he hand him a scorpion? Now, then, if you, bad as you are, are disposed to give your children useful gifts, how much more readily will the Father in heaven give the Holy Spirit to those that ask him!"

THE PARABLE OF THE GODLESS JUDGE

Lk 18:1–8: "He also told them a parable to show that they must persevere in prayer and not lose heart. 'Once upon at time,' he said 'there was a judge in a town somewhere who did not fear God and

49

had no regard for man. In the same town, there lived a widow who used to come to him and say: "See that justice is done me! Rid me of my persecutor!" For a time he refused; but later he said to himself: "I do not fear God and have no regard for man; but, at any rate, since this widow is pestering me, I will see that justice is done her. I am afraid she may finally come and beat me black and blue." ' The Master then added: 'Listen to what the dishonest judge says! And God will not see full justice done to his faithful who cry to him day and night? Will he really delay acting in their behalf? I tell you, he will see that justice is done with all speed! But, when the Son of Man returns, will he find the necessary faith on earth?' "

Christ speaks of the prayer of petition in several parables; it concerns a promise and a demand.

First of all the promise: "He who asks receives. He who seeks finds. He who knocks will gain admission." Christ illustrates this promise with the example of the child who asks for bread and certainly will not be given a stone. Or he asks for a fish and will surely not receive a snake. Or he asks for an egg and assuredly will not get a scorpion. If mere men are this good how much better is God! With an inexorable sense of reality Christ continues: "You men who yourselves are wicked give your children only what is good." He who knows about the wicked knows also about the good. He who knows the heart of human fathers knows even more the heart of his heavenly Father. God is love. A petition invoking this love will find no closed door.

But does not experience prove the opposite? Thousands of prayers remain ungranted. Wretched disappointment is the result. Do not the experiences of daily life prove the promise of Christ wrong? A favorable hearing and fulfillment are promised.

Denial and unfulfillment are the reality. But Christ adds: "How much more will the heavenly Father give the Holy Ghost to those who ask him for it!" (Lk 11:13). This is what is decisive. In prayer the important thing is not good weather, health, help in financial needs and the like but what is permanent and what is important in the eyes of God. And what is important is the Holy Ghost. This does not mean that other prayers remain unheard, rather it does mean that they find a favorable hearing only when what they request is good for the salvation of the one praying, that is, when the fulfillment is consistent with the Holy Ghost. So the petitioner should bring his spirit into harmony with the spirit of God. He should request whatever corresponds to the will of God; then he is certain of a favorable hearing.

But Christ also discusses the second aspect of the prayer of petition, the demand. "Pray, without ceasing." This too is explained through a parable. Whoever in the middle of the night asks his friend for help, and at first finds deaf ears, is heard at last if he does not give up (Lk 11:5). The situation is perfectly sketched. The friend has already gone to bed. His children are with him in the same room, not to mention the poultry and goats and sheep. A great number of things lie about. The heavy beam is pushed before the gate to barricade it. Opening would wake everyone up and cause great confusion. Nevertheless the friend will get up despite all the unpleasantness involved just to have peace again.

The same thought is pictured in another equally dramatic parable. A judge who fears neither God nor man is finally forced, against his will and contrary to all his habits, to take on the lawsuit of a widow from whom he can hope neither for

51

any financial reward nor for gain in prestige, and this wholly because the woman with her perpetual nagging gets on his nerves so much that he cannot get rid of her in any other way but by fulfilling her request (Lk 18:2). The thought is the same in both parables. One must ask again and again and not stop asking. But the right attitude consists of these two bound into unity, the vision of the promise and the fulfillment of the demand. This means constant, tireless, repeated asking, not in doubtful anxiety but in quiet confidence in God's goodness and in consciousness of the security to be found in God's love. Confidence and entreaty must be united. Then man is bound to God; then he can see everything in God's light, hope in God's goodness, receive from God's hands, use objects according to God's will and for his honor. Only then is prayer help for man and glorification for God.

The church has in its *Ritual* formulas for the blessing of all possible things: of bread and wine, of salt and water, of animals and flowers and houses, of automobiles and airplanes, of clothes and of stables. All the everyday objects of life are included in these blessings, for all should serve man and help on his way to God. And if everything is thus provided with the blessing of God from above, so too from below should everything be subordinated to God by man. Prayer is not merely unworldly contemplation, detached examination; rather everything which busies man in his day-to-day existence may and should be included in prayer: concern for house and field, for food and clothing, for health and advancement, for study and relaxation. Everything in the realm of human life should be drawn into a relationship to God through the prayer of petition. Then it is blessed from above and consecrated to God from below. Life becomes a unity in God. And piety becomes in the good sense of the word an everyday affair, because it forms each day and hallows all that happens to man the entire day. And through the correct interior attitude of prayer all this is built up and imbedded in the Holy Ghost as the most important need of man, without which all else is meaningless. Something bright, expansive, radiantly happy, loosening all crampedness and despair, making impossible every defection from God, overcoming all fragmentation, this something lies in the promise and demand of the prayer of petition as it presents itself in the parables of the lord.

Receptiveness

THE PARABLE OF THE SOWER

Mt 13:4–9: "Look! The sower goes out to sow. As he sows, some of the seed falls close to the footpath; and the birds of the air come and eat it up. Other seed falls on stony ground, where it does not have much soil; and, because it has no soil of any depth, it shoots up at once; but by the time the sun has climbed the heavens, it is scorched and, because it cannot strike root, withers away. Other seed falls among the thorns, and the thorns come up and choke it. Still other seed falls on the right kind of soil, and this at last bears fruit, in some cases a hundredfold, in others sixtyfold, in others thirtyfold. Let everyone heed what he has heard."

Mt 13:18–23: "For your part, then, listen to the explanation of the parable of the sower. Whenever anyone hears the message announcing the kingdom and does not really grasp it, on comes the evil one and steals what has been sown in his mind. Such a one is described by the words 'sown close to the footpath.' The words 'sown on the stony ground' describe one who, the moment he hears the message, receives it with joy; but he does not let it take root in himself; on the contrary, he is a timesaver and, when distress or persecution comes on account of the message, he is at once upset. The words

53

'sown among the thorns' describe one who hears the message, but the cares of this world and the deceitful attractions of wealth utterly choke the message, and it turns out to be barren. The words 'sown in the right kind of soil' describe one who hears and grasps the message; and he, of course, bears fruit and yields as much as a hundredfold, or sixtyfold, or thirtyfold." (See Lk 8:4–15.)

The second fall of man has still not come to pass. Israel has not yet rejected the messias. Therefore a cloudless heaven still shines over land and people. And therefore the voice of Jesus does not yet have the hard ring of the fighter who must break the enemy resistance, or the hammering "woe unto you" of the speech of judgment. His voice sounds warm and full and has the alluring charm of love: a sower went out to sow ...

And yet this parable conceals an almost threatening warning. Now the waves of enthusiasm swell high. But Christ also knows that an ebb follows upon this flood. He sees behind every fresh enthusiasm of morning the crisis of the mid-day and the weariness of evening. So he wishes to warn and caution in good time. The steep ascending curve of enthusiastic consecration can precipitate abruptly if a decision based on real principle does not stand behind it. And only such a consent can be called faith. His parable wishes to exact such preparation. It is not by chance that he names first of all the three groups of refusers.

First come the *insensitive*. They hear God's word only externally. The inner organ for all religious things is stunted. The word of God does not speak to them interiorly. The next world seems to them something unreal, something that does not exist for a real thinking man. The tales of the bible are nice for children but not for adults. Christianity is a crutch for cripples. Anyone who can stand on his own feet will master his life alone. Faith is an outlived conception for those behind the times, a survival from the middle ages. And after all one cannot cook soup with religion or pay rent or, in any case today, make a career of it. Muscles decide, and intelligence, and proficiency and connections, and organization and stronger battalions. All else is opium for the people. The word of God may be something to others. To them it is nothing. So it does not penetrate to the interior. At most it hits externally and glides off unobserved. The number of these insensitive persons is legion.

Secondly Christ names the *superficial*. These are the film people. All slips by them, flits around them. They are open—only too much so. They are ready to receive everything. But nothing remains fast. Nothing strikes root. They lack depth and proper resonance. They are butterfly types which sip on a thousand blossom cups. Sanguine men of the moment, today elated to the sky, tomorrow depressed to the point of death. They can cry at an open grave in the morning and dance at a wedding celebration in the afternoon. Their laugh fades quickly, and their tears dry even more quickly. They guide themselves by the fashion and swim with the stream. Their credo for the moment they borrow from the best-selling novel of the year. Their highest moral commandment is "keep smiling." Of course they are also religious, for they are time and again affected when they hear the solemn sound of church bells or listen to Beethoven's Missa Solemnis. In their living room hangs a picture of the madonna, and on their bookcase stands the Fioretti of Francis. Of course one may not subject them to endurance tests. No sacrifice may challenge their faith. In times of persecution they promptly burn their prayer-books and under no conditions let themselves be seen near a church. Then when calmer times come again whatever has been neglected can in any event be made up, that is, if religion happens to be in fashion again. And besides one does have time on his deathbed to muse on things that during life at best make one melancholy. Weathervane men, who cannot be trusted, their number is beyond reckoning.

In the third place stand the *defeated*. They have fought long and struggled honorably, for their faith was a matter of conscience for them. They received it from a good mother, developed it in religious instruction and bravely defended it in the first storms of youth. They had principles and wished to live according to them. A practicing christianity was to them presumed, a Sunday without mass unthinkable. It was no façade and no pretense but genuine throughout, vigorous and rooted. But after all one is a human being and does not live in the good old days. One must venture out. One must accomplish something professional. One must progress, must run the course in business along with the others. One must have social relations on all sides. There is little else to do except to devote one's whole time and strength to the expansion of life, to the development of the standard of living. Anyone who does not use all his strength no longer keeps up with the rest. Thus for a long time interior religion and exterior life continue alongside one another. But the exterior swallows ever more time and strength and absorbs the entire attention. The religious world becomes more colorless and weaker; it fades farther and farther into the distance, asserts itself less and less often, and in the end succumbs quietly and unnoticed of spiritual consumption. One still grieves for it occasionally, but eventually even this grave is forgotten.

Who would deny that these three groups enumerated by the

lord picture an all too sad reality? There is nothing lacking in the sower. For Christ strides over all lands and through all centuries and strews the seed of his teaching in bold sweeps. There is just as little defect in the seed. For they are the vigorous seed of God's word. But the readiness is lacking. The proper susceptibility is not there. The defect is in men.

In sudden contrast to these three groups of deniers Christ places the three groups of victors. In the first instance he discusses the *hundred percenters*. These are the complete and the integrated, the flawless, the saints. They seek first of all the kingdom of God. All else comes afterward. They live according to a correct scale of values in which God and the will of God occupy first place. All else is relegated to second and third places. All is directed toward God. They are pure unclouded mirrors which catch up the entire light of God and brilliantly reflect it. These are unworldly men who travel through the anteroom of this life unconfused, whose feet nowhere linger, who stride with bounding, brave steps out of the dark gloomy valleys into the light. They seek and find God in everything. Everything becomes to them a glorification of the lord. For the joys of life they are grateful to the eternal proclaimer of the good news. And when they have to suffer they know that it is the Father in heaven who sends them the chalice whose drink tastes so bitter, but like a medicine also strengthens and heals the soul, so that for it too they praise the Father who is in heaven. They are the men of great fruitfulness. Outwardly they seem desirous of accumulating failures. In reality, in their hands all things work toward eternal life. They bear full sheaves into the granaries of God. They are the men of spiritual fullness, the serene spirits and great hearts, the daring souls who have gambled all on one card. They win the game.

The men of sixtyfold fruit are also praised by the lord. Shadows flicker in their lives. They have their setbacks. They return wounded from the battle. But they have won. The light has become stronger than the darkness in their lives. And it has in the end separated all masses of clouds and insured the perpetual spring. They are not saints of obvious holiness. They are struggling and maturing. Often enough their breath threatens to give out as they swim against the stream. But they have repeatedly looked to God and turned to God, have repeatedly cooperated with grace. In this way their land has become ripe with grain, and they rejoice on the day of harvest.

Even the third group, *the men of thirtyfold fruit,* is contemplated by the lord with joyful words of recognition. Their christianity was off and on from day to day. Their religious life had its tides, its low points and high points, its setbacks and progress. Bright days alternated with dark nights. It was not at all clear that they would persevere to the end. Their environment had stuck to them. Only slowly did they scrape from their feet the sticky, muddy, clodlike masses. But they had held on to Christ and had confidence in him. His words were their light, his grace their strength, his splendor their hope, his church their ark in the deluge. So they come to the shores of God and see in amazement that the lord has blessed their work.

The groups who answer "no," the refusers, the closed and encrusted, and the groups who answer "yes," the open, the prepared, stand opposite one another. The outer activism of the one is fruitless, the unpretentious life of the other is laden with fruit. Grace is offered to both. Both are fields on which the seed of God falls. But only one is ready. Readiness is everything.

The Invitation to Dinner

THE PARABLE OF THE WEDDING FEAST

Mt 22:2–14: "The kingdom of heaven reminds me of a king who prepared a wedding feast for his son, and sent his servants to bid those come to the festivities who had received invitations. But they refused to come. So he sent other servants, with these instructions: 'Take this message to those who have been invited: Consider, please, that I have finished the preparations for my dinner; my beeves and fatted calves are killed; in short, everything is ready. Come to the wedding feast.' But they carelessly went their several ways, one to his farm, another to his business; the rest laid hold of the servants, and maltreated or killed them. Then the king, in a fit of anger, sent his troops to put to death those murderers and lay their city in ashes. He then said to his servants: 'The wedding feast is ready but the persons invited to it did not prove worthy. Go, therefore, where the streets issue into the open country, and invite to the wedding feast as many as you find.' So the servants went out on the open roads and brought together all they found, bad as well as good, so that the wedding hall was filled with guests. But when the king came in to look at the guests, he noticed there a man who was not wearing a wedding robe. 'My good sir,' he said to him, 'how did you come in here without a wedding robe?' The man was struck speechless. Then the king said to the servants: 'Bind him hand and foot, and throw him into the darkness outside.' There it is that weeping and gnashing of teeth will really be heard. After all, many are invited, but few chosen."

Christianity is no innocuous affair. Grace is of course the greatest offering that ever has been made or will be made to a man. But a refusal is a refusal of God and therefore necessarily of most grave consequence.

The parable of the wedding feast illustrates this point with perfect clarity. Jesus is not concerned with some pleasant celebration but with the wedding of the crown prince, therefore a most solemn state occasion which would take place only every few decades. An invitation thus means a special token of distinction, and a refusal is lese majesty, which the king cannot accept silently. Christ is the only-begotten son of God. In his incarnation he comes to call his bride, the holy church, to the wedding, and to invite men to the feast. The parable lists four groups of invited guests.

The first group are the *disinterested*. To God's invitation there is also such a response. The invitation goes forth to them several times with accented urgency. But religion says nothing to them. They are realists for whom only the earthly and material is a reality. The ideal is to them a luxury which they do not know how to approach, good for do-nothings who do not know that time is money. The businessman is here for business. He knows that he must use his time to secure his position and to improve his economic situation. Christianity does not interest him. It does not belong in his world. It has nothing to do with speculation in stocks, bank business, professional advancement and social position. The invitation remains lying on his desk unanswered or finds its way into the waste paper basket. In reality however there can be no indifference to God, for God does not permit it. Whoever does not trouble himself about Christ does not enter into the kingdom of God; he is one who stands outside and accordingly remains outside. The final judgment of the lord will be "I know you not!" Those remaining outside belong in the end with the rejected.

The second group are the *men of the opposition*. In the parable they quickly kill the bearer of the invitation. They have respect neither for the ruling lord nor for the heir to the throne. Their proceedings are thus a political action, the expression of a revolutionary disposition. They stand unequivocally in the other camp. The act of force is an expression of their attitude. Concerning the kingdom of God they are the militant atheists, the haters of christianity. Religion is for them no indifferent matter but an opium for the people, a hindrance to the rise of mankind, a drag chain on social development, an enemy of true humanity, a restraining remnant of the superstitious middle ages which must now be finally liquidated. So they carry on the battle in words and writing, they join together in common action and organize the opposition. In the parable the answer of the king is not long in coming. His troops surround the stronghold of the enemy opposition, raze it to the earth and annihilate the enemy. It is a metaphor of the great reckoning of Christ at the end of time. The apocalyptic images of the destruction of Babylon and of the annihilation of all of satan's followers are the application of the penal expedition in the parable to the reality of the kingdom of God.

The third group are the *disrespectful*. The parable describes a single figure as their representative. The man who was invited to the wedding from the street and who had been offered a wedding garment in the anteroom is convinced that his rags are good enough, that he should be accepted as he is. The invitation means nothing special to him. In the spiritual sense it refers to men who are not really interested in knowing about God. The fear of God is lacking in them. They know nothing of reverential awe. God is for them one thing alongside many others. Religious life is something to which from time to time, more constrained than willingly, one gives expression. Attending mass on Sunday morning is like going to a restaurant for lunch or to a concert in the evening or to the office on a weekday. God should be happy when they trouble themselves about him. And the church may congratulate herself when they accept her invitation to worship. These are the men who have never correctly grasped deep inside themselves what a call of God means. The difference between creator and creation, eternity and time, infinity and finiteness, lord and servant has for them never become truly vital. They speak of religion as one speaks of politics, business and sports. And so they take absolutely no pains to develop a corresponding inner attitude. They do not perceive that a christian lives differently from a nonchristian. Because God is for them something incidental, they do not trouble themselves to ask whether they are living in the grace of the lord or in sin. They are external members of the church, citizens in the kingdom of God, guests at the wedding. Within, in their thoughts and loves, in spirit and in conviction, they do not belong to Christ. The result is drawn drastically in the parable. It is expulsion out of the illuminated banquet hall into the darkness, out of freedom into chains, out of election into rejection. External membership in the church of Christ does not suffice. If the inner transformation does not occur the final result is rejection.

The fourth group are the *real wedding guests*. They are of course a remarkable collection: tramps, vagabonds, proletarian folk, beggars and do-nothings from the highways and byways. The invitation was the great surprise of their lives. Joyfully they complied. With trembling awe they crossed the threshold of the palace, with childlike joy put on the wedding garment given them, and now they are at the wedding feast as in heaven. Only one thing do they fear: ever again to have to go out into the filth and into the misery, out into the cold and darkness. These are the men with shining eyes and thankful hearts, the men who know what grace and vocation are. It is the man of sin who is called into the world of grace. It is the religious man who knows that without God everything is nothing, who knows how to appreciate the call as a freely given grace, and who bears the painful discovery of his own weakness and sinfulness deep within himself. But all loses itself in the splendor of festive joy, for he knows that christianity is the wedding feast which had its beginning at the incarnation of God and will reach its full festive height at the second coming of the lord with a light which will nevermore be quenched and a joy which will nevermore fade.

So Christianity demands a decision with a pro or con, a yes or no. It is no more innocuous than God. It is concerned with the final and most profound question: eternal being or nonbeing.

THE PARABLE OF THE BANQUET

Lk 14:16–24: "Once upon a time, a man planned giving a great supper and sent out many invitations. About the time set for the supper he sent his servant to give notice to those invited: 'Come, everything is now ready.' Then all alike proceeded to beg off. The first said to him: 'I have bought a farm, and I must of necessity go and inspect it. I beg you, consider me excused.' Another said: 'I have bought five teams of oxen; and I am just going to try them out. I beg you, consider me excused.' Still another said: 'I just got

63

married, and for that reason I cannot come.' When the servant returned, he reported these excuses to his master. The head of the house flew into a rage. 'Go out quickly,' he said to his servant, 'into the streets and lanes of the city, and bring in here the poor and crippled and blind and lame.' Again the servant reported: 'Master, your order has been carried out, and there is still room for more.' The master then said to the servant, 'Go out on the highway and among the hedges, and compel people to come in. My house must be filled to capacity.' I tell you, therefore, not one of those originally invited will taste my supper."

The invitation to dinner is a sign of special confidence, a kind of admission into the intimate family circle. The gospel speaks therefore with striking frequency of banquets. It was on such an occasion that Christ worked his first miracle. His great farewell speech was spoken at a dinner gathering. At table he showed himself again to his disciples after the resurrection. It was at a meal that he allowed the disciples at Emmaus to recognize him. The worship of the primitive church is the community of the love feast and the eucharistic meal. For the enduring union of Christ with the christian is that community which is accomplished in the love feast of the eucharist. The Sunday worship is the remembrance and renewal of the farewell meal and of the sacrificial meal at the same time. So it is not surprising that Jesus also compares the eternal life with a great banquet. To a group gathered around the table he spoke the words: "Blessed is he who partakes of the meal in the kingdom of God." But at the same time he also related, to the surprise of all his dinner companions, a parable of who is to be found at that meal and who not.

Those who refused are described first. They are primarily those who live in luxury and therefore have no need of religion. "I have bought a farm and I must inspect it." These are the men who are self-sufficient. Life overwhelms them with its goods. So in this external abundance they scarcely come to perceive their inner emptiness. One house-ball follows another, one garden party follows another. Saturday night celebrations which last into the Sunday make impossible attendance at worship on Sunday morning. These men have nothing against religion, but personally they get along without it. Material riches stifle the consciousness of their spiritual poverty.

The second group are the *much occupied*. "I have bought five teams of oxen and must try them." Time is money. Sunday must also be used to visit business friends and prepare for the coming week. In the economic race only he who knows how to use his time can keep up. Religion is good for women and children, and of course in old age one will personally come back to it. But now one's profession demands one's entire energy.

The third group are the men of *sensuality*. "I just got married and can therefore not come." Too often these men allow their sex urge to drown any other call. Rather than make use of sex the way God willed, they make sex itself a god. Needless to say, our lord was not condemning the holy sacrament of marriage, but only those who misuse sex, who make of sex an obstacle to divine grace rather than as one of the most sacred and intimate means of union with God.

In all three groups it is materialism which keeps men at a distance from the kingdom of heaven, whether it exhibits itself in the fine or crude form. The Spirit of God is shoved aside by material gain, advantage and enjoyment. God is relegated to

65

second place, or even to no place at all. These men have heard the call, but they have excuses and more important things to do.

But the portrayal of those who accept is still more unusual than the picture of those who decline. There are two groups. The first group comprises the *beggars, cripples, blind and lame*. The men from deprived environments, the injured, the beaten, those marked by fate are more susceptible to the call from above. They have nothing to hope for from the earth and look more quickly to heaven. This world brings them only affliction. So they hope in the eternal which should bring them happiness and blessedness. Suffering is a plowshare tearing up the field of the soul. Need recognizes religion as the needed.

Is religion then only a crutch for the crippled? Solace for the fallen? By no means! In his sketch Christ intends to portray not only and not primarily bodily misery. He is thinking of the spiritual "beggars." They are the men who are conscious of their spiritual poverty and know that the decisive thing is grace, for which man as beggar can only ask. Self-conscious superiority is self-deception. Humble knowledge of one's own wretchedness is truth. For this reason it is the spiritual mendicants who are called to the lord's banquet.

The cripples are the men who know about the workings of sin. Whether or not he perceives it, whether or not he confesses it, man cannot of himself judge rightly in the decisive questions, and cannot always choose correctly. He is directed to God's grace and strength. Thus he knows the crippledness of fallen man and seeks salvation and healing from the outstretched hand of God.

The blind are the men who know that we can know nothing. For if we look to our final end, into the light of God, we are at first completely blinded. If one sees only the earthly one is blind to God. But one cannot see God without dying. Whoever does not know of his own blindness is deluded.

The lame are the men who know that one can walk God's path only with God's help. "Without me you can do nothing," says Christ. What is the good of walking with great strides and in stepped-up tempo if it is not on the path of God! Whoever has this insight is ready for God's word and works. He understands the grace-character of christianity; he will comply joyfully with the call to the banquet of the lord.

The second group are the men "from the highways and hedges," the outsiders. Like the people of Israel of old, these residents of the house of God exclude themselves through their "no." And the gentiles, who were outside, are called in and will "sit at table with Abraham, Isaac and Jacob." The same thing is true today. Not every baptized catholic and externally traditional christian is really inside the house. For on the tree of the lord there are also withered twigs and barren boughs. And many who externally and apparently stand outside, but have the right attitude in their hearts, are in reality within. They have, as the theologians say, baptism of desire. They stand, as seen by humans, outside at the hedges and fences of the church. But seen by God they are within, because they obey the inner call of the voice of God.

Thus the banquet of the lord is a realization of the mysterious words of Christ that the first shall be last and the last first. It is not the external, social order of precedence which is valid before the eyes of God but the completely different inner order of grace. What will be seen as men gather around the table of the lord for his banquet will bring great surprises.

67

Right Attitude

THE PHARISEE AND THE TAX COLLECTOR

Lk 18:10–14: "Once upon a time, two men went up to the temple to pray, the one a Pharisee, the other a tax collector. The Pharisee stood conspicuously apart and soliloquized this prayer: 'O God, I thank you that I am not like the rest of men—robbers, rogues, adulterers— or like that tax collector over there. I fast twice a week; I pay a tax of ten per cent on every item of my income.' The tax collector, on the contrary, kept in the background and would not so much as raise his eyes to heaven, but struck his breast and said: 'O God, have mercy on me the sinner.' I assure you, this man went down to his home acquitted of all guilt; not so the other. Everyone who exalts himself shall be humbled, and he who humbles himself shall be exalted."

The parable of the pharisee and the tax collector is immortal. The two images are too dramatically presented, their profiles too sharply chiseled for one ever again to forget them.

That the pharisee is unsympathetic needs no proof. Pose is always laughable. Snobbishness always repels. Commercial profit and loss calculation in the religious life is always grotesque. If piety then degenerates still farther into arrogance toward God and proud presumption toward fellow man it changes into its opposite, and the "righteous" becomes in its innermost being unrighteous. The pharisee is a man whose life seems to be completely formed and permeated by religion. From morning until evening he anxiously follows all the prescriptions of the law of God. He performs the ritual washings conscientiously, observes all the food prescriptions, does not take one step more on the sabbath than the law allows. He wears the prayer phylactery without any regard for human respect, prays at the ordained and prescribed times, fasts more than is necessary, pays the tithes of all that is prescribed and yet more besides. Thus he leads a hard life, confined by a thousand stipulations, all for the sake of religion.

But he has two flaws. First of all he is very conscious of his religiosity and holiness. When he prays it is only a thanks for what he has and is and not a request for what he has not and is not. His fault is his belief in his faultlessness. He admires himself. The second mistake is related to this first: he despises the others. He judges and condemns them. For he is convinced that he stands high above the others. He is a self-righteous man who unrighteously condemns the others as unrighteous.

In present circumstances it would be easy to find this pharisee frequently in God's house, and of course always in a visible place. His genuflections are flawless. He sprinkles holy water in all directions. In devotions his voice is clearly audible. If a preacher scolds about unbelievers, communists and others outside the fold he nods approvingly. He never eats meat on a Friday. His bookcase is filled with prayerbooks. And everyone knows that he constantly carries a rosary in his pocket. But even today he would be conscious of his own holiness and blamelessness, and no word would be sharp enough for his thorough condemnation of filmstars, sun bathers, girls of doubtful character and beatniks and every kind of "atheist."

But the tax collector? He has a bad conscience. And rightly so. Time and again he has transgressed the law. He must continually associate with gentiles professionally; without a lax conscience he could not even perform his duties. In the temple he is far from feeling at home. Seldom enough does he wander in there, and quickly enough does he leave again. When he bows his sinful head, strikes ruefully on his breast and begs, "Lord, have mercy on me the sinner," it is only too warranted. But there is good in him too. He is conscious of his sinfulness and does not fancy himself to be something before God. Never yet in his life has he considered himself pious. Holiness is an ideal which he recognizes, but from which he knows himself to be personally far distant. In short, a sinful but honest soul. But is he not also, fundamentally, completely repugnant to our sensibilities? This hypocrisy, this head hanging, this whining at his own sinfulness, this bowing and scraping, this shaking at the knees! From mere inferiority complex he dares not look up once. He does not have the courage to walk to the front. True humility does not fear to expose itself. A person of upright character stands by his actions and takes the consequences as they come. If this tax collector has the same attitude outside the temple, in his family or in his profession, as here in the holy place he will be completely incompetent in life, unable ever to head a family and a large household. He will never be able to raise his sons as upright men of character. He will never get on in his profession. It is dead certain that he will be ridden under.

The decisive factor is not the external posture. One person can kneel in the first pew, conscious of his poverty within and therefore pressing to the front to the source of grace. And another can stand in back under the gallery, at the church door with a heart full of conceit and with proud disdain for all others. Not the exterior posture does Christ portray but the interior bearing of the disposition of the heart. Only he who knows that God alone is holy and that the sanctification of men comes only through his grace will be sanctified by God. Conceited self-complacency is only sanctimoniousness. Christ chiseled the two types sharply that our examination of conscience might lead to a definite judgment. The external does not matter. What Christ wishes to sketch here is the contrast between false self-consciousness and true grace-consciousness.

Man must know that he is oriented entirely toward grace. All that he does is senseless, worthless and, in the eyes of God, meaningless if he does it only of his own strength. Christ says expressly: "Without me you can do nothing." Thus the amazing words of Augustine: "The virtues of the heathens are brilliant vices." The basis lies in that other statement of Christ: "Only one is good: God." Our action is good then only when it proceeds from the grace of God, is accompanied by the grace of God, is brought to conclusion by the grace of God. Then there is something godly in it, and it is good in the eyes of God. Our thinking is merely a thinking-with, our going is a going-with, our working a working-with. If man in a promethean arrogance wishes to fetch the fire from heaven himself, if he prides himself on his actions in order to brag, then the very truth and reality will prove him wrong. The proudest babylonian tower of technical knowledge, of science or art, of commerce, of politics, of the entire culture is in the eyes of God nothing if it is not borne and animated by the grace of God. Besides this consciousness of being mere creatures and with it the absolute dependence on God something further must be added. Man must recognize and acknowledge that even in this thinking-with, going-with and working-with he constantly fails; in other words the consciousness of being a sinner must become vital. God draws the plan. We can only carry the diagram out, not even doing so of our

71

own strength; and in the process we bungle things. We can play only accompanying music, and not even of our own power; and here too we produce disturbing dissonances again and again. The honest man knows of this failure. The greater his insight, the more honest his character, the clearer his thought and the more consistent his inner attitude the more serious, the clearer and deeper is the consciousness of man's sin. So human life becomes an ellipse with two focuses: God's grace and man's sin.

But now the decisive factor: the grace of God is really given, provided that man has this consciousness of dependence and sinfulness. When this grace is given to him he can work, he can proceed, he can build and form. His work will then be good, his actions sensible, his life meaningful before God. When therefore man enters into this spiritual relationship of consciousness of contingency and sin before God, then grace will be given to him by God. He comes to God weak. He goes home strong. Poor in soul he comes to God; he goes home rich. He comes to God empty; he goes home overflowing. It is the attitude of Paul: "I can do all in Him who strengthens me." It is the attitude of the psalm: "In your name I leap over the wall." The real attitude which a christian should have is then the attitude of the tax collector who, returning home from the temple, upright, filled with strength, beaming with joy, laden with energy, exuding vitality, inspired by determination, seizes his task and masters his life. No more presuming on his own strength—he is aware at bottom of its failure—but unconditionally trusting and presuming on the grace of God, on the strength of the almighty. In this disposition the basis is withdrawn from any pride, every conceit is excluded, every arrogance is banned. Moreover in this disposition all inferiority feelings are also overcome, all weaknesses are healed, all failures are made good. For human weakness is compensated and surmounted by the strength of God. Therefore the deportment of the christian is the deportment of the tax collector returning home from the temple, according to the words of the apostle: "Through God's grace I am what I am."

THE ATTITUDE OF THE TAX COLLECTOR

Lk 18:23: "The tax collector, on the contrary, kept in the background and would not so much as raise his eyes to heaven, but struck his breast and said: 'O God, have mercy on me the sinner.'"

Luther's question: "How do I find a gracious God?" presents itself to every religious person. For when he stands before the holy God, thinks honestly and sincerely, he must be conscious of his sinfulness. And he is immediately tortured by the pressing recognition that the sinner cannot of himself make things good and bring about order. If he nevertheless makes this attempt his theoretical recognition is corroborated through painful experience. So only one thing remains: the appeal to God's grace. The sinner knows that he is arraigned before the court of God, knows that if all goes according to justice and law the death sentence will fall. But now the unexpected happens. Jesus Christ comes forward for the accused. For Christ has himself made atonement on the cross. For the sake of his intercessor the indicted sinner is now acquitted by the judging God. The acquittal however is at the same time an emancipation. For the word of God is true and cannot assert that the sinner is a just man if he remains a sinner. The word of God moreover has creative force. It is an effective word, for it effects the new being and the new life of

73

grace. Sin therefore is not merely covered up but is blotted out. Thus it is said of the tax collector: "He went home justified." Man is through Christ in no way simul justus et peccator, at the same time sinner and just. For righteousness and sin are contradictions and oppositions which cannot exist in men at the same time. No dialectic can help out here. Man is either a sinner or justified. He is not both at the same time. So when it is said: "He went home justified," it is meant thereby that he is no longer a sinner. A really creative change has been accomplished in him. He goes home another man, not merely externally and not merely in the judgment of God but also interiorly and in reality. Justification signifies that for the sake of Christ the sinner is made truly just through God's grace.

Sin then does not remain in man as reality, but sinning as a possibility continues. Thus man must cooperate in forming himself. Justification is an operation of God. But the cooperation of man is included and enclosed within it. Negatively this means that man should sin no more; positively it signifies that he should cooperate with the grace received. He should now live as a just man. The justice which he has received should through a union of God and man result in the reorganization of life.

Three things are required:

1) Man must recognize and confess his sinfulness before God.

2) He must appeal to the gracious God, must beg for grace through prayer.

3) He must cooperate with grace in order to lead another, new life, or more precisely, to guard and to bring to development and into operation the new life which he receives.

Each of us is this tax collector. Anyone who does not admit this is a pharisee, one who becomes a sinner only through self-justification. But for all of us who see ourselves in this tax collector the entrance to grace is open, for Christ has removed the barricades through his death on the cross.

Thus the parable of the tax collector is comfort for everyone who is aware of his own sinful existence. The pharisee has only an exterior, an apparent justification founded on his own conceit, and at most on the judgment of men, and which in this case is a false judgment. On the other hand his hypocrisy is condemned by the God of truth. The tax collector condemns himself but finds grace before God, and with it a judgment of acquittal. The pharisee who pardons himself is condemned. The tax collector who condemns himself is acquitted. For it is not the judgment of man himself but the judgment of God which decides. Therefore we can win the verdict only if we go to God as the tax collector did.

Deeds

THE PARABLE OF THE UNLIKE SONS

Mt 21:28–32: " 'Once upon a time a man had two sons. He went to the first and said: "My son, go and spend today working in my vineyard." He acquiesced and said: "I will, sir." But he did not go. He then went to the second and told him the same thing. But he refused and said: "I do not want to go." In the end, however, he felt remorse and went anyway. Which of the two complied with his father's wishes?' 'The last-mentioned,' they replied. Then Jesus said to them: 'I tell you frankly: the tax collectors and the prostitutes are ahead of you in entering the kingdom of God; for, although John's mission was strictly within the limits of the law, you did not believe him; but the tax collectors and the prostitutes did believe him. You saw what happened, but in the end you did not feel remorse and believe him.' "

75

In the parable a father sends *his son* into the vineyard to work. The son answers "yes" but then he does not go. And as though the yes does not sound polite enough he adds: "Yes, sir," implying that he wishes to acknowledge unreservedly his obvious conformity to the higher will. With this image Christ pictures the hypocrisy of the leaders of Israel. They know the will of God from the law and apparently conform to it when they pray in the synagogue, sacrifice in the temple, celebrate the feasts and observe the law. And yet it is only show. The decisive factor does not materialize. Inner conversion and selfless working deeds are lacking.

There are also such men in the church of Christ. Their religion is mere theory; it is not put into practice. They are blossoms without fruit, words without deeds. What good are iron resolutions when the realization is lacking? Of what use are ingenious projects without execution? Programs which remain on paper? Talk of principles which sound impressive but are not put into practice? What good is the bible on the bookshelf and the leatherbound missal in the hand if conversion of the heart does not take place? The most magnificent encyclicals and episcopal pastoral letters are of no avail if this catholic teaching does not awaken catholic life. Clever essays and theologically sound books on asceticism and mysticism are empty noise without the corresponding deed. A piety which is only literature is hypocrisy. Only the demonstration of life matters. Words are too cheap. The devout first son of the gospel finds no grace before God.

The second son answers "no," but then he goes into the vineyard and works after all. He is exteriorly a rude fellow whom every command provokes to opposition, a man who is inclined to contradiction and apparently does not know what filial piety is. But behind the coarse crust flows a good juice, and the hard shell conceals a sweet kernel. With him talk always comes somewhat before thought. But then when the thought follows it affects his actions. And this is decisive. There is lacking in him exterior devotion of word and bearing, but he has the true inner surrender of preparedness for the action. In the parable it is the apparently impious who in reality seek God: tax collectors and whores who sin through their refusals but then afterward go and reform themselves. There are many such men. Big words do not interest them. Long prayers do not suit them. If one were to ask them about the way to purgation, to illumination and to union they would not know how to answer. They have no idea of the various ascetical schools and directions. Biblical quotations are unknown to them. Among the pious they are considered black sheep. They use rough language and answer most of the time with "no." But deep within they have a correctly functioning conscience. And time and again they discern the truth and have the courage to draw out the consequence. In the end one can rely on them. In times of persecution they are numbered among the loyal.

Is this type the ideal? Certainly not! For christianity knows no cleft between theory and practice. It therefore promotes no theory which does not correspond to practice, but also no practice which contradicts theory. It wishes no great gap between word and deed. Words without deeds do not count. But deeds in contradiction to words are inharmonious.

Therefore behind the gospel's story of the first and second sons there looms mysteriously the figure of the third son, who says "yes" and also acts correspondingly. Any "no" to the word of

God is foreign to him. He lives in both theoretical and actual readiness to say "yes" in both word and in deed. He is the restless, striving, constructive man. He is the antithesis of the "spirit who constantly contradicts." His whole life is a single "yes, lord." He is the son of man and son of God, the son absolutely. His incarnation is the "yes" to the will of the Father in heaven. His prayer and his speech are the yes in word, his life even in all details is the yes in deed. And both word and deed are solemnly sealed and proved genuine through the yes of the sacrifice, the last surrender on the cross. Before he stepped over the threshold of his passion he said: "Father, not as I will, but as you will." To this affirmation he remains true even to the last breath and to the last drop of his blood.

The ideal christian attitude is thus the bearing of this third son with whom all remonstration and rebellion, all resistance and contradiction, all spirit of opposition and all personal ambition are overcome through resignation to the great and holy will of the lord. It is not an enforced, resentful resignation. Still less is it a submission out of weakness, the line of least resistance. Rather it is the strong, courageous growing out of oneself and into the greatness of the divine will. It is the affirmation of love which shows itself in deed and life. Not the impetuous, devout yes-sayers whose inaction deprives their cheap words of any weight and seriousness, not the obstinate, sulky and defiant no-sayers who must be converted anew each time before they finally laboriously come round to the act: rather it is the great men with a clear attitude of preparedness for the word and will of God who are the true and complete christians. It is the attitude which is to be found mysteriously between the lines of the parable and which has found its ideal realization in the lord who speaks the parable—in him who as logos is the word of God, the affirmation of the will of the Father.

Rejected

The parable of the wine growers *who slay the son and heir is a warning to the leaders of Israel and a sign of the history of this people which finds in Christ its fulfillment which is inverted through their refusal.*

THE PARABLE OF THE WINE GROWERS

Mt 21:33–44: " 'Once upon a time there was a landowner who planted a vineyard, set up a fence round it, dug a vat in it, and built a tower; he then leased it out to vinedressers and went abroad. When the harvest season drew near, he sent his agents to the vinedresser to receive his share of the vintage. But the vinedressers seized his agents, beat one of them, killed another, and stoned a third. So he sent another group of agents, more numerous than the first; but they treated them in the same way. Finally, he sent to them his own son, saying: "They will respect my son." But when the vinedressers saw his son, they said among themselves: "This is the heir; come, let us kill him and seize upon his inheritance." So they laid hold of him, drove him out of the vineyard, and killed him. Now, then, when the owner of the vineyard returns, what will he do to those vinedressers?' They said to him: 'He will put those wretches to a wretched death. And besides, he will lease the vineyard out to other vinedressers, who will give him his due share of the vintage at its proper season.'

"Jesus continued: 'Did you never read this Scripture text:
"The very stone which the builders rejected
has become the capstone:
this is the Lord's own doing,
and it is a wonderful sight for us"?

79

For this reason I tell you: the kingdom of God will be taken away from you and turned over to a nation that will produce the fruits expected of it. He who dashes against this stone will be crushed; and he on whom it falls will be ground to powder.' "

The history of the people of Israel runs on outwardly like the histories of other peoples. Wars, revolutions, dynastic struggles, court intrigues, physical progress and severe setbacks alternate with one another. After a sharply climbing curve the highpoint is reached under David and Solomon. But then the irreversible decline sets in. Thus all appears to happen according to the laws of development which decree the fate of all peoples. And yet Israel's history is different. Israel is the chosen people of God. It is a vineyard which Yahweh has laid out and planted— as Ps 79 pictures with inimitable beauty. God has given the people the land, the law, the temple, the ritual and great men. But the vineyard must bear fruit. So God sends the prophets to bring home the fruit, in the northern kingdom an Elias and Eliseus, an Amos and Osee, and in the southern kingdom an Isaias and Jeremias. And even in exile there come forth Ezechiel and Daniel and the others. But the prophets suffer the fate of prophets. They are laughed at and slandered, persecuted and killed. Then comes the hour of decision for the people. God sends his own son, his beloved, the anointed. Will Israel understand the hour of grace? But the chosen repudiate him who has chosen them. They exclude him from the community of their and his people, and they kill him "outside the city" on Golgotha. He is thus the rejected. They have been commissioned to build the temple of God and have discarded the son of God as an unusable stone. But he is and remains the cornerstone which should bear and hold the entire structure. The plans of God fulfill themselves without Israel and despite Israel. They who have rejected him are now themselves rejected. God chooses the gentiles for his new stones. And on Christ as the cornerstone the new Israel, the spiritual temple of God, the holy church is erected. The vineyard is taken from Israel and given to the gentiles that they may cultivate it and deliver to the lord the fruits of love. This is Israel's inner history. It is chosen by the lord, rejects the lord and is itself rejected.

The history of this people is a warning for all men and peoples.

Grace is offered to every man. For "Christ enlightens every man that comes into this world" (Jn 1). Only if the one chosen refuses and rejects this grace is he himself rejected. But God's plans do not therefore miscarry. He chooses others and realizes his intentions in them. Peoples too have their hour of grace, their times of decision. If they repudiate Christ they themselves will be repudiated. But the erection of the universal church nevertheless goes on without them, for others are called. The light is removed from that place. Grace is at the same time responsibility. The yes to Christ is the way of ascent for men and peoples. To say no is to go down the steep incline; it is the beginning and cause of their own rejection. Men and peoples prosper because of Christ. But men can also be ruined because of him, depending on whether or not they follow his call. The parable of the vinedressers is an indication of the fates of men and peoples and shows the inner secret of history and its real meaning, alongside of which the entire external course of events becomes completely incidental. We must learn to see correctly.

THE PARABLE OF THE TALENTS

Mt 25:14–30: "Furthermore: imagine a man who, before going abroad, sent for his officials and entrusted to them his money. To one he gave five talents, to another two, and to a third just one—to each the amount proportioned to his individual ability. He then went abroad. At once the recipient of the five talents went to invest them in enterprise and made another five. In like manner, the recipient of the two talents made another two. But the recipient of the one talent went away to dig a hole in the ground and buried his master's money. After a long delay the master of those officials returned and settled accounts with them. So the recipient of the five talents came forward and presented five additional talents. 'Master,' he said, 'you trusted me with five talents; look, I made another five.' 'Well done, my good and faithful servant,' the master said to him; 'you were faithful in managing something small; I will now put you in charge of something great: share to the full your master's happiness.' When the recipient of the two talents came, he said, in turn: 'Master, you trusted me with two talents; look, I made another two.' 'Well done, my good and faithful servant,' his master said to him; 'you were faithful in managing something small; I will now put you in charge of something great: share to the full your master's happiness.' Finally the recipient of the one talent came before him and said: 'Master, I know you are a hard taskmaster; you reap where you have not sown, and you store away what you have not winnowed. So I shrank from doing anything at all and went to bury your talent in the ground. Here you have your capital back again.' But his master had an answer for him: 'You lazy, good-for-nothing fellow!' he said to him; 'you knew that I reap where I have not sown, and store away what I have not winnowed! Then you ought to have put my money in the bank, and on my return I might at least have recovered my capital plus the interest. Therefore take the talent away from him and give it to the one who has the ten talents. Every man who already has will receive yet more till he abounds in wealth, while the man who does not have will lose even what he has. And as for that unprofitable official, throw him into the darkness outside.' There it is that weeping and gnashing of teeth will really be heard."

Slave life in the orient was by no means necessarily synonymous with primitive life and hard manual labor. There were slaves who filled high offices. These too are found in the parables of the talents and the minas which sketch the rich man who goes on a trip and in the meanwhile leaves his property to a few slaves to administer. After his return home the reckoning ensues. The judgment sounds at first unusual. The first slave, who received five talents and doubled them, lays a sum of nearly $12,000 on the table for his lord. The second received two talents. He too can present with pride about $4400. The third neither lost nor increased his $1200 and merely hands it back to the lord. The judgments for the first and second are precisely alike, but for the third it is crushing. The judgment of the lord looks not to the absolute but the relative result, not on the measurable product but on the work and exertion which were made. The first and second doubled their sums and consequently made the same effort, and accordingly they receive the same reward. The third made himself comfortable and did nothing, hence the punishment.

With God it is exertion, not the result, which is decisive. This is on the one hand consoling, for there is nothing required of man other than his own personal contribution, his sincere effort to work with what has been given him. It does not depend on us how much we receive. But it does depend on us what we do with it. On the other hand this parable holds the serious warning to exert ourselves and cooperate. Man therefore works out his salvation not alone through grace, and not alone through his actions, but primarily through grace, and only secondarily through his own cooperation.

Of course whether we have received capabilities such as

83

health and strength of the body, intellectual ability, good pre-dispositions of the heart and character, good upbringing, or whether we receive supernatural capital through special grace does not lie in our hands. God is the sovereign, free lord who distributes as he wishes. But the decisive thing is that we get the full value out of what we have received, work and create with it, untroubled by the outcome, which is not most important and often does not lie at all within our power.

This attitude seems to contradict the statement in the epistle to the Romans that not the willing and the running decide but rather God's mercy (1:16). And yet it is no contradiction. For the same Paul writes in the first epistle to the Corinthians that we must exert ourselves in the contest of life like the athletes in the stadium. And Paul consequently demands both: the merciful grace of God as primary, but also the contribution of one's own strength and exertion as secondary. Only the synthesis of the two results in the correct christian attitude. If one has received little he should not complain but work and create with the little according to his strength. Then he is certain of his reward. If he has received much the responsibility grows with what he received and he must make a corresponding contribution. Mere passivity is condemned. Man is not a vacuum which merely takes grace receptively; he is a living being who received grace and then must follow it and cooperate with it. Whether it is a question of the inner enlightenment of the spirit, the stimulation of the will, the demand of the conscience or the proper grace of the sacraments the cooperation of man is always required. In this parable lies something dynamic, active, creative. It is an appeal and summons for men. And behind the whole stands the ac-count that is rendered in court. God is the lord; we are the servants. He has distributed his gifts diversely. Our task is to work with the gifts. For this and only this task must we submit an account. On this and only this task depends the judgment.

THE PARABLE OF THE UNSCRUPULOUS MANAGER

Lk 16:1–13: "Once upon a time, there was a rich man who had a manager, and complaints were made to him about this man that he was letting his estate go to rack and ruin. So he summoned him and said: 'What is this I hear about you? Submit your balance sheet! You can be manager no longer!' The manager then reasoned as follows: 'My master is taking the management away from me. What shall I do? To dig I am not strong enough; to beg I am ashamed. Ah, I know what to do, so that, when I am ousted from the management, people will welcome me in their homes!' And calling his master's debtors to appear before him, one by one, he said to the first: 'How much do you owe my master?' 'One hundred jars of oil,' he replied. 'Take your note'; he said to him: 'quick, sit down and write fifty.' 'And you,' he said to another, 'how much do you owe?' 'Eleven hundred bushels of wheat,' he replied. 'Take your note,' he said to him, 'and write nine hundred.' And the master commended the unscrupulous manager for his shrewd way of acting.

"The fact is, in dealing with their own kind, the children of the world are shrewder than the children of the light. And so I say to you: money is a worthless thing; but use it to make friends for yourselves, so that, when it gives out, they may receive you in the everlasting homes. He who is conscientious in small things is conscientious in big thing also; he who is unscrupulous in small things is unscrupulous in big things also. Therefore, if you do not prove conscientious in handling so worthless a thing as money, who will trust you with a genuine good? And if you do not prove conscientious in handling what is not your own, who will trust you with what is your own?

"A servant cannot be the slave of two masters; for either he will hate the one and love the other, or, at least, be attentive to the one and neglectful of the other. You cannot have God and money for masters."

85

In the parable of the unscrupulous manager a man commits fraud regularly. Promissory notes are falsified. And the whole affair ends with praise for the manager, "because he has behaved shrewdly." Is the parable then a hymn to the immoral? Does the end justify the means? Some commentators have sought to eliminate the difficulty by asserting that the tenant has such power of attorney according to jewish law. But this excuse does not help; moreover there is no problem involved at all. What Christ wishes to say is simply the following:

The children of darkness are refined and cunning in the use of their means to achieve their aims and often enough do achieve their immoral goals through the cleverness of their procedure. So too the children of light must seek to obtain their moral goals with their moral means just as cleverly and just as zealously. It is therefore neither goal with goal, nor way with way, nor means with means that is compared; rather *the point of comparison is the exertion which is made and should be made on both sides*. And with regret it is substantiated that the exertion of the wicked is often greater than the exertion of the good. The opposite of course should be true. If one wishes to be still more specific then one can read into the parable that the children of darkness are concerned with getting. For the manager who is too lazy to work and too superior to beg arranges through his forgery maneuvers to secure the necessary income for himself. The children of light on the other hand should not be concerned with getting but with giving. Through this giving they should use this money that otherwise will certainly be used for an unjust end in making friends. For those to whom it is given will be intercessors for those who give, so that the gates of the eternal home will open for the benefactors. Thus the parable is a demand for real serious contribution, for giving, donating and helping. Helping love is true cleverness. Self-centered shrewdness is clever only in the eyes of men. But the incredible thing is that men so often confuse light and darkness; they see before them men who through refined methods arrive at an unearned income, and consider these methods beautiful and bright ideals, whereas these people are in reality dark, sinister characters who despise others as mere shadows because they do not understand how to accumulate property but are convinced that it is more blessed to give than to receive. The lives and thoughts of christians and nonchristians are opposites. Man must decide; he cannot "serve God and money." Either his life is in the service of God, in which case he cannot pay homage to money, or he is a servant of money, in which case he can find no grace before the living God. Many shirk making their decision and hope to sneak through by way of a compromise, and with materialized christianity and a christian materialism to have their cake and eat it too. They wish to join the craftiness of the children of darkness with the shrewdness of the children of light. Through a lax and elastic conscience they attempt to incorporate immoral transactions in their christian credo. They drive on two tracks and use double bookkeeping.

OF THE UNFRUITFUL FIG TREE

Lk 13:6-9 "Once upon a time, a man had a fig tree planted in his vineyard. He came to look for fruit on it, and did not find any. So he said to the vinedresser: 'It is now three years since I have been coming to look for fruit on this fig tree, and have not found any! Cut it down! Why, really, should it impoverish the soil?' But the man pleaded with him. 'Sir,' he said, 'let it stand one year more. In the meantime, I will dig up the ground around it and put in manure. If after that it bears fruit, well and good; if not, you may have it cut down.' "

Two forces apparently collide with one another: God's justice and God's mercy.

God is just. He cannot therefore tolerate sin, be silent about the fruitlessness of his creature, simply cover with the mantle of love things which contradict his will.

God is merciful. Therefore he cannot measure everything with the scales of justice; he is silent to much, takes into consideration the weakness of men and lets his sun shine not only on the saints but also on the sinners.

A seeming contradiction. The parable of the fig tree gives the answer: God *is* just and so he demands fruit—demands it inexorably. And if there is no fruit the tree is cut down. The inevitability of divine claims appears in this parable. The seriousness of being called and summoned lies upon man. It is placed on him as a task which he must fulfill. He is called to give account. He cannot therefore do with his life what he pleases. He cannot act as if he himself would ordain everything. He cannot idle away his days in indifference. He must bear fruit.

But God is also merciful. So he gives man time to bring forth the required fruit. Mercy means that God waits with the judgment of his justice and in the meanwhile gives man a chance, and of course gives him this chance in such a way that he is helpful to him in this interim. The tree in the parable is given better soil. It is fed with manure so that it will not lack fruit.

Mercy thus signifies God's waiting and helping, but only during the time that is allotted to man. When this time is run out justice has a free hand. Then the time for mercy is past. The seeming contradiction between God's justice and God's mercy lies only in the fact that we with our short-sightedness suppose that all must be resolved now in the short timespan of this world. The solution however lies in a chronological sequence, in a period of mercy now and in judgment in justice at the end.

The parable is valid in the first place for the *people of Israel.* God planted this people in the good earth of the promised land, gave it all manner of help to bear its spiritual fruit: the temple, the law, the prophets. And now this people has a last chance through the coming of the messias. This last chance is at the same time a very special aid. If this decisive last period of grace goes by unused the fate of Israel is sealed. The tree will be cut down.

But the parable is also valid for each *christian.* He is planted in the earth of the church through baptism. His life is given divine help through the guidance of the church, through the sacraments, through the word of God, through inner light and inner strength. If his life has been unfruitful until now then he always has another chance. Christ enters on his behalf. And thus the sin is not immediately avenged. He has time for conversion, time to cooperate with the grace of Christ and thus to bring forth the fruit that God demands and expects. But there comes the time when the period of grace has run out and man is delivered up to the justice of God.

The parable is also valid for peoples. They too have their times decreed by providence, the proclamation of the gospel, the means of sanctification of the church, the models of the saints, the works of good men. They have their ordained, God-given time and period. When this time has run out the judgment will fall.

Something uneasy, threatening lies in the mystery of the exacting justice of God. And yet at the same time something consoling, benign lies in this parable of the patient mercy. Thus the christian life is menaced by justice but upheld by grace. It moves in the twilight of the preliminaries of this world until it ends according to circumstance completely in light or completely in darkness.

Love above All

THE PARABLE OF THE MERCIFUL SAMARITAN

Lk 10:25–37: "Presently an expert in the Law came forward to sound him out. 'Rabbi,' he said, 'what must I do to obtain a place in eternal life?' 'Well,' he replied, 'what does the Law say about it? What do you read in it?' He answered: ' "Love the Lord your God with your whole heart, and with your whole soul, and with your whole strength, and with your whole mind"; and besides, "Love your neighbor as yourself." ' 'Your answer is correct,' he said to him; 'act accordingly, and you will have life.' But, being anxious to justify his question, the man said to Jesus, 'And who, pray, must I consider a neighbor?'

"Jesus complied with his request and said: 'Once upon a time, a man who was on his way from Jerusalem down to Jericho fell in with bandits; they stripped and beat him, and then went their way, leaving him half dead. By some chance a priest was going down the same road; but when he saw the man, he made a detour. In like manner a Levite came near the spot and he, too, made a detour at sight of him. Finally a traveling Samaritan came near him, and he, on seeing the man, was stirred to pity. He went up to him and bound up his wounds, pouring wine and oil into them. He then

90

mounted him on his own beast of burden and brought him to an inn, where he took care of him. Moreover, on the morrow he produced two denarii to pay the innkeeper, and left these instructions: "Take good care of him; and in case you spend anything over and above this sum, I will repay you on my way back." Now which of these three men seems to you to have taken a neighborly interest in the man who had fallen in with bandits?' 'The one,' he replied, 'who pitied him in that practical way.' 'Very well, then,' Jesus said to him, 'model your conduct on his.' "

The question asks: who is my neighbor? The scribe, or expert in law, had of course only asked it in order to elude the somewhat painful concrete challenge through a flight into theoretical discussion. But the question is always being formulated and has a meaning for all men of all times. Jesus' answer is: your neighbor is every man who is in need, even if he apparently is the most distant stranger. Destitution makes the most distant stranger a neighbor.

Two illustrations prove this point. The first is the parable of the samaritan. The man between Jerusalem and Jericho really appears to be the most distant stranger. But he is in need, and indeed so much so that he can no longer help himself. For the robbers have not merely completely despoiled him but have also beaten him half dead. He can only with difficulty attract attention through movements and call for help with a weak voice. Priests and levites who pass by can rightly claim that this man does not concern them. They have good excuses at their disposal, grounds by which they can excuse themselves from the demands of conscience. The priest rationalizes that this corporal work of mercy is not of his office. For there is in every ordered community a

91

division of authority and distribution of offices. Order is insured when everyone does that for which he is commissioned and not something else. The cobbler must remain at his last, the priest at his altar. The soldier must fight and the housewife must cook, and not the other way around. Besides, officiating at religious ceremonies is no mean thing. It is the highest office and so this official must keep himself free for his important function. In the consciousness of this importance he passes by. The levite has just as valid a reason for going past. As a levite he has in a special way the task of caring for levitical purity, and whoever touches a dead person is levitically unclean. But one cannot know whether this half dead man who moans for help might not die in one's hands and make one legally unclean and thus render participation in the service of the temple impossible. Hands off, then! The law of God stands above sentimentality. The levite holds to the letter. Worrying about the spirit he leaves to others. He goes past in the consciousness that he has just overcome a temptation and fulfilled a duty.

The traveling merchant is different. He would have the best excuse at his disposal. For he could say: 1) This half dead man is a stranger, a foreigner. For I am of Samaria, he of Judea. Between the two of us there are tense political relations. To help an enemy would be treason. 2) This sufferer is a member of another confession, for he prays to God in Jerusalem, we on Gerizim. 3) He does not concern me professionally. I am a merchant, have my business to manage and am neither doctor nor nurse nor policeman. 4) As a businessman I must consider my own profits. But this work of mercy can only incur losses for me. It would cost me time and money and strength, would dirty my clothing and bring me to disrepute. 5) The deed would be dangerous, for the robbers may be hidden somewhere nearby, lying in wait for me too. To spur the horse and gallop away would be the most sensible solution.

Then the unexpected happens: conscience wins. This man climbs from his horse; he does not merely organize help from a superior distance, he does not go off to seek assistance somewhere else, but he personally puts his hand to it. He lifts the wounded man to his horse. He leads him with care by the bridle to the inn. He brings the half dead man to security. He puts up money for him and gives a carte blanche to the innkeeper for possible expenses. This wounded man was of himself the most distant stranger to him. But because he was in need he viewed him as a neighbor and showed him the love of a neighbor. Thus the most distant stranger becomes through destitution the neighbor. Model your conduct on his!

Wherever pressing need is visible, excuses must cease. All barriers must be overcome. Barbed wire must be cut down, trenches must be filled up, walls must be torn down. All prejudices must be shoved aside, unpleasantness must be accepted. There are no works of mercy without unpleasantness. It does not matter whether men are suffering physically or spiritually, financially or morally, intellectually or religiously. And no barrier, either political or social or confessional or racial or any other, is valid. The most distant stranger becomes the closest neighbor. Need must construct a bridge and overcome all distances. This is the first level.

Jesus exemplifies the second level not through words but through his life. Mankind lies half dead between the spiritual Jerusalem of paradisal happiness and the Jericho in the lowlands of satanical enmity, because the enemy, satan, has robbed it

93

completely and beaten it, leaving it half, though not completely dead. Grace is lost, man's supernatural riches plundered, the strength to recognize God and to do good weakened. The entire situation is such that humanity can no longer help itself of its own strength. Self-delivery as an illusion, return to an earthly paradise an hallucination. The priests of all possible human religions, cults, philosophies and schools of salvation go by. They occupy themselves only theoretically with the problem of evil. The levites with exterior works of mercy through physical healing and training, through material betterment, organized planning, technical mobilization of natural forces likewise miss the decisive point. They wish not to profane the purity of their discipline and the objectivity of their method through religious practices. The situation would have been hopeless if he who stands at the greatest distance had not come: the distant God. And indeed he has come to those who were really for him the most distant, to sinful man, distant not merely through the difference of creator and creature, infinite and finite, eternal and temporal, heavenly and earthly, but distant most of all through the "no" of sin, through the conscious turning away, through the fall into the subhuman, through the surrender to the satanic. But God comes to this half dead humanity through his incarnation in Jesus Christ. He binds up its moral wounds through the oil of his words and the wine of his sacraments. He lifts it to be carried by the horse of his grace. He brings it into the church, that protecting inn along the highway of the millennia, and promises that he will put in order all that is still lacking on his return at the last judgment. Thus is he the great samaritan who throughout all history lifts up mankind. He is the personal, lived illustration of his parable of the most distant stranger whom love makes the neighbor because it does not know distance, but instead brings the distant near.

To us our neighbors are often far distant because through self-love we pay attention to them. To the real christian on the contrary the most distant must be near because love sees everyone who suffers. Self-love makes distant; love brings near. Therefore love is necessarily love of neighbor—it knows no stranger.

THE PARABLE OF THE MERCILESS SERVANT

Mt 18:23–35: "The kingdom of heaven reminds me of an earthly king who, once upon a time, desired to settle accounts with his officials. In the course of the settlement one who owed him ten thousand talents presented himself; and since he had no means of paying, the master ordered him to be sold with wife, children, and all he had, and payment to be made. Then the official went down on his knees and, prostrating himself before him, said: 'Have patience with me, and I will pay you everything.' Touched to the heart, the master of that official canceled his debt and set him free. But no sooner had that official gone outside than he met one of his fellow officials who owed him a hundred denarii; and, grasping him, he was about to choke him, saying: 'Pay what you owe.' Then his fellow official went down on his knees and pleaded with him: 'Have patience with me and I will pay you.' But he would not hear of it; on the contrary, he went and had him thrown into prison until he should pay the amount owed. Naturally, his fellow officials, who saw what had happened, were deeply grieved; and they went to their master to tell him all that had taken place. Then the master summoned him. 'You merciless man,' he said to him; 'I canceled that whole debt of yours because you pleaded with me. Was it not proper for you, too, to take pity on your fellow official just as I had taken pity on you?' And with indignation his master turned him over to the jailers until such time as he should pay the whole debt. In the same way my heavenly Father will treat you if you do not each forgive your brother from your heart."

The relation of man to God must determine his relation to his fellowman. This is a general law of christianity. For this reason the Our Father pleads: "Forgive us our debts, as we forgive our debtors." And the lord tells us: "With the same measure with which you measure out to others, will it be measured to you." And the demand of Christ remains, that we should learn from our Father in heaven who lets his sun shine upon good and evil and bestows his rain on sinners and saints.

The parable of the merciless servant applies this law to a single case of forgiveness. As God forgives us so must we also forgive. If we do not forgive he also will not forgive us. But this parable places the comparison of the vertical relation of God to man and the horizontal relation of man to man in the right proportion. In the parable the merciless servant owes his lord more than ten million dollars, while his fellow servant owes him only the modest sum of twenty-five dollars. There exists therefore no proportion. The debt which is remitted to the servant is so monstrous that the triviality which he now had to remit his fellow servant is just plain laughable. An offense against God is through the infinity of the offended person so great that the offense of man against man cannot compare with it. And yet we men again and again think the other way around. Being wronged by a man seems to us unbearable, while we make little of our wronging God through our sins. The screaming misproportion of the two numbers mentioned in the parable has something shocking and disconcerting about it.

We have wandered far from the norm. We no longer place the relation with our fellowmen in connection and in comparison with our relation to God. We have made of religion so much an affair merely of the internal that the external relations to our milieu and to our fellowmen are no longer correctly seen as a religious matter. We have removed God and the world both in principle and in fact so far from one another that our relation to God no longer affects our relation to the world. We believe that our various connections with worldly affairs must be regulated by their own proper laws and have nothing to do with religion. Thus religion is confined to a small snippit of life, to a mere sector in the entire circle. By this confinement it loses its strength to form life and the world anew. And so it happens that an entrepreneur considers himself a good christian because he fulfills his religious duties, and yet at the same time he is unjustly holding down and suppressing the pay of his employees and workers. Or it can be that a christian housewife faithfully fulfills her Sunday religious duties and at the same time manages her employees at home roughly and unjustly. She is a lamb before God, a dragon before men. Or religious men swear their love to God in pious devotions and then just outside God's house talk about and criticize their fellowmen uncharitably. Workers and employees can be very zealous in their church life without ever thinking that they are obliged by this very religion to be conscientious in their secular duties and in their work. To the man who thinks correctly on religious matters this discord and dissonance become a scandal, whereas the men who are falsely oriented in religious matters are not conscious of this disparity at all. We must again place the earthly and human in its relation to God. We must again unify our religious attitude; only then is the parable fulfilled in its proper meaning. If we do not then we are threatened by the judgment, which is drawn in the parable with inexorable harshness and severity. We are servants of God for whom God has remitted the vast debt of sins, and we are therefore obliged to

97

remit to our human fellow servants the little that they owe us. We are children of God, sons of the Father in heaven. Therefore we must show our fellowmen, who as children of the same heavenly Father are our brothers and sisters, the same love which we ourselves receive from our Father in heaven. We will never be able even remotely to measure out according to the standard by which good is measured to us by God. But we can at least keep in mind that even if the proportion fails the obligation as such remains.

Attitude toward the Earthly

THE PARABLE OF THE RICH FOOL

Lk 12:16–21: "Once upon a time there was a rich man whose land yielded an abundant crop. So he soliloquized as follows: 'What shall I do since I have no place to store my crops?' Finally he said: 'This is what I will do: I will pull down my barns and build larger ones; and there I will store my wheat and all my goods; and then I will say to myself: My good fellow, you have many possessions laid up to last for many a year; take life easy now: eat, drink, and enjoy yourself.' But God said to him: 'You fool! This very night your soul will be demanded from you: who is then going to get what you have provided?' It is the same with anyone who hoards to indulge himself and does not think of God in amassing wealth."

Never before has man spoken so much of security, and never before has man lived in such insecurity as today. We seek to secure ourselves financially by buying every possible kind of insurance: against accident, burglary, hail, fire, illness, etc. The insurance companies are in full bloom and for their part cover themselves through reinsurance. And we have protected the entire nation in its old age through social security. We protect ourselves physically through hygiene, sports, vitamin rich nourishment, vaccinations. Individual position is secured through joining professional organizations which are intended to preserve, protect and further our interests. Thus the individual is protected by the mass. We are secured politically through armed forces, through treaties and an entire system of pacts.

And still there remains insecurity, which is connected at one time or another with everything human. Despite everything one actually feels uneasily the fragile floor on which the entire structure of security rests. Everything human is fleeting and thus offers no final and lasting security.

Christ speaks of this fragility in the parable of the rich fool. This man has managed his affairs brilliantly. To secure himself he keeps everything for himself, builds large granaries, lays in provisions, piles up riches and creates for himself the feeling of security. But God tells him: "You fool, this very night your life will be demanded of you!" The real basis of insecurity is thus the transiency of human life. The certain fact of death gives all else the character of the uncertain. Modern philosophy also proceeds out of this certainty of death and from it opens up the question of the meaning of human existence. If we exist only in order to die not only this existence but with it also all human action is brought into question. Every attempt at security is unmasked as illusion. For death will certainly shove all security aside.

Should life then be lived in insecurity? This attitude too was and is in part today still in vogue. Nietzsche, who in his innermost soul hated all bourgeois security, summoned man to insecurity and challenged him to travels on new seas and the climbing

of new summits. Mussolini presented the idea of vivere perico-
losamente to an entire people as an ideal. And a false heroism
wishes to proclaim as a matter of principle an affirmation of
human insecurity as alone of value. But Il Duce was slain by
his perilous life of danger, and Hitler's wandering dreams of
security brought a future of insecurity not only upon the german
people but also upon entire Europe. Must the thought of death
force one to come to terms with the insecurity of everything
human, and as a consequence either suffer passively in insecurity
or assent to this condition knowingly? Christ's answer is completely different. He concludes the parable with praise of him
who is "rich in the eyes of God." Thus in the words of Christ the
two deciding points in the question of security are named with
unsurpassable precision: death and God. Death as the power
which shatters all human security. And God as the force which
offers the only security. Christianity teaches: do not trust in
human security, whose uncertainty is demonstrated by death, but
also do not live in uncertainty with question marks behind everything; instead trust in only one thing, in God. In him there is
absolute certainty and security.

To verify this truth visibly Christ summons an elite to voluntary, conscious surrender of all human security in order to be
secured in God exclusively and alone. He demands of this elite
complete surrender to God through abandonment of possessions
in voluntary poverty; he requires renunciation of human security
in the marriage community through voluntary chastity; he de-
sires the renunciation of the security of the personal ego and
demands in its place the surrender in obedience. And alongside
this elite Christ demands of all who bear his name that they seek
their final security only in God. What is faith other than building

upon the word of God, even where verification by the human spirit is not possible? What is consciousness of grace but the admission of the insecurity and inadequacy of human strength and human act in order to ask for the decisive strength and security from God? What is the reception of the sacraments but the recognition that there is no certainty of salvation and sanctification in men except in Christ, who has given us the sacraments as the means and paths of salvation and sanctification? What is the church but the teaching that there is no final place of security in a human community, but only in the community of the redeemed and in and with Christ? What is the other-worldly perspective of the christian except the logical consequence of the fact of death, which is for us not an end but a new and decisive beginning, a striding out of the anteroom into the banquet hall, out of the twilight into the light?

God's words: "You fool, this very night your life will be demanded of you," are valid for the man who has built upon human and consequently false securities and now in the earthquake of death sees all his towers crash. But they are not valid for the man who has sought his security in God, who alone is secure. Security in insecure men is folly. Security in the certainty of God is wisdom.

Of the Camel and the Eye of the Needle

This is not a parable but a metaphor. But it is so memorable in its formulation and so meaningful in content that it cannot be overlooked or omitted.

Mk 10:23–27: "Then, looking round, Jesus said to his disciples: 'Oh, with what difficulty will those who have the goods of this world enter

101

the kingdom of God!' The disciples were dumfounded at his words. But Jesus took occasion to repeat his statement: 'Children, how difficult it is for those who put their trust in worldly goods to enter the kingdom of God! It is easier for a camel to pass through the eye of a needle than for a rich man to enter the kingdom of God!' They were completely bewildered and said to one another: 'In that case, who can be saved?' Jesus looked straight at them and said: 'Where man fails, God still avails. God can do all things.' "

Even the wording is effectively sharp, and the content is a candid summons to battle against the modern world.

1) Let us begin with the formulation. "It is easier for a camel to pass through the eye of a needle than for a rich man to enter the kingdom of God!" One of the largest animals through one of the smallest of openings: the impossibility can scarcely be expressed more dramatically. Already we can see pedantic quibblers putting on their pedagogic spectacles, wrinkling censoriously their parchment colored foreheads and admonishingly lifting their fleshless hard fingers of righteousness to announce their protest against such extravagant and overstated assertions. O you dusty, tedious criticasters! Gnaw your lips and chew on your thousand pencils. Despite all Christ does not bind himself by your elegant and refined grammar! His flashing spirit breaks new paths everywhere; he does not move in the traditional trot of your bourgeois diction. He loves just such keen formulations: "You swallow camels and strain out gnats." "You see not the beam in your own eye." "Pluck out your eye and cut off your hand if it causes you scandal." "You are a race of adders and a brood of snakes." These are sentences which stand like quivering swords of flame in the gospel. The words of God are no tender flowerbed, no neatly clipped ornamental plants in hothouse nurseries, but giant firs

defying storm and weather. They are no artistically fitted mosaic floor for gentle fountains but gigantic mountains reaching steep into the heavens. Always great, always gigantic, always defiant, always stimulating. The speech of the prophets and the harsh flashes of Paul's words resound in the same way. Christianity is no Babbitt affair but a struggle between God and devil, death and life, heaven and hell. For Christ has not come to bring peace but the sword, not the dressing gown but the armor of God. Thus the gospels are no Pollyanna tales for the harmless but cutting knives, rolling thunder, convulsive earthquakes in the world of the spirit. Pedantic souls will be embarrassed by the gospels.

Still sharper is the contradiction made by the sentimental, the languishing, the gaudy. These persons do not express themselves directly. Their only salvation is to pour as much water as possible into this fiery wine of Christ. His dangerous maxims are rendered harmless. They explain that the eye of a needle is not the eye of a needle but a low, narrow gate in Jerusalem through which it was just barely possible for a camel to squirm. Even today they lack proof that this gate actually existed and was actually referred to in the speech in Galilee. Then, not being able to explain away the eye of a needle, they attempt to make the camel smaller by explaining that there is a similar sounding word which in English means a ship's line. This is of course correct, and as a result the clumsy camel is deleted from the world of the gospel; but nothing is thereby changed. For a cable cannot go through the eye of a needle. The impossibility remains. And with it remains the impressive speaking manner of the lord, who also used the "impossible" image of swallowing a camel. But just such speech they find offensive. For to speak of camels and of the pains of a woman in labor (Jn 16:21) and of the emptying of the

103

bowels (Mk 7:19)—that is certainly too strong. Where is the unction? Where is the odor of incense? Where is the prayerbook style? And after all, is it not unwise to compare the rich with camels? There may be consequences. We are, are we not, determined by economics? Money rules the world now. And even catholic undertakings must be somehow financed. So it will be far better to skip lightly over this painful sentence or cover it up with a pious deluge of words, or seek to file away all the corners and edges through skillful commentary so that it rolls through the sermon without opposition like a smooth ballbearing.

Still more painful is the opposition of the hardnosed heresy-hunter who digs around every little sentence which does not appear completely secundam Lucam. It is a pity that Christ expressed himself so precisely, otherwise they would have drawn a menacing question mark with red ink in the margin next to such sentences and incorporated the entire scriptures in their dossier of heresy-suspected writings. Would Christ not have done better to limit himself to the smooth words of the catechism or the theologically certain formulations of Denziger and explain along these lines: "If anyone say that inner attachment to money is compatible with God-willed selflessness, let him be anathema!" The language of the textbook alone seems to them sanctifying. Camels and eyes of needles are not at all suitable as means for the illustration of religious truths! Above all one should, according to their interpretation, eliminate from religious books everything which is in any way audacious. An imprimatur for such books is justified, in their opinion, only if no new thought is found therein. And they bestow a special decretum laudis if all the statements have already been expressed elsewhere, and with the same formulation. Then tradition is secured.

Of course we need skilled theologians who watch responsibly over the purity of teaching, and one should not in any way advocate dogmatic daredeviltry. But one must know how to distinguish between textbooks of scholarship and writings of popular preaching. Each has its own language.

In truth this statement of Christ about the camel and the eye of the needle is a path breaker. He blazes a trail for the language of preachers and orators, writers and lay apostles, who do not preach the gospel in clerical gown and stole from distant high pulpits, but bear it into factories and offices, into lecture rooms and railroad compartments and wish to speak the language of our time and our men. There must be more blood in our preaching, a greater closeness to life and a greater sense of reality. This spirit burns in the gospel page after page. But the bearers of this message spread so many ashes over it that one can scarcely feel the glow anymore. Give our orators, writers, artists, opinionmakers freedom for their formulations! We can learn this lesson from the bible. The message of God walks before man in all possible garments. It rejoices in songs and psalms, mourns in gripping lamentations, thunders in powerful speeches, rings out in splendid hymns, hammers in original aphorisms, flashes in bold theses, entices and warns, threatens and weeps in the pauline epistles, teaches in balanced doctrinal chapters, instructs in historical presentations, wonders with the great eyes of children, cries in the wild tumult of the people. The book of Job could almost be staged just as it is, so dramatically is the action built. The little books of Esther and Ruth read like delightful novelettes, Tobias like a travel novel. And how daring and bold are the images of the canticles! How astonishing, almost offensive seem many of the visions of the prophets. In thousands of forms and

105

formulations the word of God speaks to us. Yet how enmired and confined we are today in our artistic shaping, in our diction, in our forming of symbols! How stereotyped are our expressions! Let the architects calmly go new ways in encompassing space. Let the artists make new attempts in forming symbols! What do the phoenix and the pelican say to people today? How little all of this affects today's life, how little it has grown out of today's perceptions. And do not lay every word a gifted orator or struggling writer tells us of the soul of modern man upon the gold scale or under the microscope of the Inquisition. Are the rigid religious forms really pertinent to today's life? Is our religious music born of the hearts of our generation with its hopes and yearnings, its mourning and weeping? We need freedom for formulation, lest in the end the gospel be proclaimed only to the "pious," no longer to the seekers, and least of all to those in the hedges and fences.

Truly the edged, pithy, succulent metaphors of the camel and the eye of the needle rustle like refreshing rain on the dried ground of all pedants, sweep like a wild storm into the glum corners of sentimental halleluja piety, and vibrate like sharp lightning in the sultry atmosphere of the scrupulous so intent upon orthodoxy. One breathes again more freely, strides again more joyfully, sings again more cheerfully after reading such a biblical text.

2) If Jesus uses such sharp words and so drastic an image, he must be concerned with a serious matter. But possession of earthly goods seems to be such a permissible, harmless, completely indifferent matter. What does it have to do with the kingdom of God? But in just this seeming harmlessness of the affair lies the danger. The exterior neutrality unexpectedly becomes a camou-

flage of inner dependence, a sedative of an uneasy conscience, a stupifying opium for vigilant christians. Therefore the urgent warning voice of Christ: "Woe to you, you rich!" Therefore the apparently exaggerated words: "It is easier for a camel to pass through the eye of a needle than for a rich man to enter the kingdom of God." Is it not peculiar that Jesus speaks so often and so urgently against human attachment to money and riches, while he really speaks seldom of unchastity and sensuality? But temptations to unchastity, perverted impulses of sensuality are less dangerous for man insofar as he immediately recognizes them as erroneous, unpermitted and perverted, while attachment to material possessions, as Ignatius demonstrates in a famous meditation in his *Spiritual Exercises,* spins itself gently like fine thread around the human soul, and then only slowly, little by little, before man even realizes that he is already half caught, becomes a net of self-seeking and in the end a wrought iron chain of Godless pride.

What then should be the attitude of a christian toward possessions?

If one wishes to understand the teachings of Jesus on earthly possession, one may not tear a single passage out of context, may never build upon a mere single text, but rather must survey and include all the pertinent statements of Christ. Then the following picture presents itself in a few strokes:

1) Possession in itself is not evil, and it is therefore not condemned by Christ.

Jesus counts among his disciples also the rich Nicodemus, the well-to-do sisters of Bethany, the rich Joseph of Arimathea and the financier Zacheus without demanding of them that they should give away all their possessions. To the rich young man

107

who wishes to know what is necessary for attainment of eternal life Christ enjoins simply the keeping of the ten commandments. He can aspire to the kingdom of heaven therefore without having to sacrifice his riches. When in the Acts of the Apostles it is stressed that the first christians held all things in common (Acts 4:32), it is also emphasized in the same context that this apportionment was not demanded or obligatory but completely voluntary, born of pure idealism (Acts 5:4).

It is thus false to judge primitive christianity a proletarian movement, and incorrect to see in uncompromised christianity some form of communism. The tenth commandment: "Thou shall not covet thy neighbor's goods," survives too in christianity. The legitimacy of private ownership and possession is the basis of the economic order also for the christian. If religious marxists consistently maintain the opposite they are only introducing their own ideas into the bible, or relying obstinately on one or another isolated text instead of really studying the *entire* biblical teaching.

But is not the camel of the gospel enormously diminished and the eye of the needle unwarrantedly enlarged through this emphasis on the permissibility of possessions, so that the passage is no longer so difficult and a miracle of God no longer required to get such a miniature camel through a billboard eye of a needle? No! The difficulty remains in full force. For:

2) Christ demands unconditionally and with uncomfortable seriousness the *inner freedom* from every possession.

Christianity is essentially an ethics of disposition. Therefore christian reform does not progress from outside in, from the institution to the spirit, but again and again from within out, from the spirit to the form.

So too in social life. For this reason Paul can write: "Who is a slave remains a slave." Is this sabotage of social development? Condemnation to perpetual backwardness, perpetuation of impossible social relationships? Nothing is farther from the truth. One must be sure to include the second concept that this same Paul stresses in the spirit of Christ: there is no longer free man and slave, and the slave is free through God. And the lords of this world should know as christians that the lord of lords has come, not to let himself be served but to serve others; that to serve is in the eyes of God therefore to govern, and to govern should be to serve the people. This completely inner transformation of the spirit, this change of disposition will then slowly renew the social order, step by step, in organic development, not in violent overturn, in spiritual evolution, not in destructive revolution.

This is true of politics too. The words of Christ: "Render to Caesar that which is Caesar's," are valid certainly for the roman Caesars, and therefore for Nero and Caligula as well. It is the acknowledgment of legitimate authority in contrast to seditious intentions and to rebellious revolt. Does it speak of defenseless surrender to every tyranny? Of abject knuckling under to the hand of the strong? By no means! For another text of the bible is also valid: "One must obey God more than men," the magna charta of freedom of conscience against every oppression. And besides this there is that text from the epistle to the Romans telling us that political power is God's servant for the common good (Rom 13), that earthly power finds its proper place within the power of God and so finds for itself divinely appointed limits and restrictions. And the Caesar will become a christian and know that the first shall be last and the last first, know that he has received his strength from God in order to do good, to help and to serve. Thus the christian spirit will create a new political order.

The same holds true for economic life. Its primary goal is not to change property relationships, but to change the attitude toward possessions. The change of attitude is a starting point for a better economic order. Here Christ applies his lever with all his strength and all his weight. Over and over he stresses inner freedom in the face of earthly, material possessions. He shows the transiency of the earthly, that treasure which is consumed by rust and by moths (Mt 6:20), on which one should therefore not set one's heart. He shows that riches can all too easily become thorny briars among which the sprouting seed of the new spirit threatens to choke (Mk 4:18). He illustrates how riches enervate men and make them hardhearted. And he refers to the correct spirit when he says in the sermon on the mount: "Are you not *anxious* what we will eat, what we will drink, with what we will clothe ourselves?" It is also the sentiment which stands in the center of his conversation with the rich young man. Hence the words of Jesus: "How difficult it is for one who has placed his trust in money to enter into the kingdom of God!" The hindrance is not having money but trusting in money—this is the incorrect inner attitude. Time and again it is this same thing which is elaborated upon as inimical to God, as dangerous, as irreligious and unchristian.

This demand of Christ for inner freedom in the face of earthly possessions is in fact a summons to battle against the modern world. Where does the stepped-up tempo of today's work rhythm come from if not from the auri sacra fames? Whence comes the mad course of our economy, the brutal dog-eat-dog politics, the unmerciful crush of competitors, the hysterical cry of advertisements, the frantic outbursts with every stock fluctuation, the suicides in monetary crises, bankruptcy and declarations of insolvency? Whence comes all this except from the convulsive clinging to possessions? Thousands upon thousands of men have bound themselves entirely to their possessions. Money has become an idol to them. And so they are unfit to enter into the kingdom of God. At most God has meaning for them in that he must help them to become rich, and must protect and preserve them from financial catastrophe. He is thus not the lord of their life but the servant. In the choice between mammon and God they have chosen the former. And certainly such men are as little able to enter into the kingdom of heaven as the camel is able to go through the eye of the needle. It is they who are referred to. When the nineteenth century, especially in marxism, raised the primacy of the economic to a principle, relegating all else to merely a light, airy superstructure built upon the economic, it set up this dependence on material goods as a dogma of our time. Thus it is essentially antichristian. Therefore the babylonian towers of our culture must crash, the chaos must come, the west must become a field of ruins if the conversion of the spirit, the reform of intention, and christianity itself do not make themselves felt with all possible force.

Thus the christian teaching on property rounds itself out to a complete whole: the legitimacy of property is preserved and secured. It unreservedly stresses inner freedom in the face of possessions. And an elite of men who also free themselves externally of all goods should keep this inner spirit constantly alive. For man will then use his money not for idolatrous worship in egoism but for divine worship in the christian way of life.

Anyone who believes that he has this inner freedom should

111

begin to do good in the grand manner, to be a Maecenas for spiritual endeavors, to help the needy on all sides. Then he will see to his surprise that his inner freedom is in a deplorable state. The camel and the eye of the needle will suddenly stand threateningly before him. What then? Then he should begin to become a christian. For "all things are possible in God."

THE PARABLE OF THE RICH REVELER
AND OF POOR LAZARUS

Lk 16:19–31: " 'Once upon a time there was a rich man who dressed in purple and fine linen, and feasted sumptuously day after day. Close by the portal of his mansion there lay a beggar named Lazarus—a mass of sores! And oh, how he should have liked to satisfy his hunger with the mere refuse from the rich man's table! Not only that: even the prowling dogs would come and lick his sores. Eventually the beggar died and was carried by the angels into Abraham's bosom. The rich man also died and was buried. Finding himself in extreme torment in hades, he raised his eyes and saw at a distance Abraham with Lazarus in his lap. So he called out: 'Father Abraham, take pity on me and send Lazarus to dip the tip of his finger in water and cool off my tongue; I am in agony in this flame.' 'But remember, my son,' replied Abraham, 'that you received all you cared for during your lifetime, while Lazarus, for his part, was in misery. At present, he is here in bliss while you are in agony. And in addition to all this, a deep chasm is once for all fixed between us and you, so that no one who might wish to cross from here to you can do so, nor can any that are there come over to us.' He then said: 'I beg you therefore, Father, to let him go to my father's house; for I have five brothers; let him give them solemn warning; otherwise, they, too, will come to this place of extreme torment.' But Abraham replied: 'They have Moses and the prophets; let them listen to these.' 'No, father Abraham,' he replied, 'but in case somebody comes to them from the dead, they will mend their evil ways.' But he said to him: 'If they do not listen to Moses and the prophets, neither will they be convinced if a dead man rises.' "

At the first reading one is tempted to interpret the parable of the rich reveler and the poor Lazarus as meaning that the rich man must be charitable and the poor patient. But there is nothing of this in the parable. Though it can be found in some translations that Lazarus would gladly have been satisfied with the scraps from the table of the rich man but no one gave them to him, this last, "No one gave them to him," is a later interpolation which is not found in the original text. But what is more important, there is in the speech of Abraham not the slightest indication to be found concerning the patience of Lazarus and the hard-heartedness of the rich man. The parable is therefore not concerned with these.

Or is the parable simply proletarian resentment against those who have and a sympathizing with all those who have not? Is it the flaming torch of social revolution? A reaction of the short-changed? Or is it rather a cheap consolation of the next world and thus a drugging opium for the stupid masses? The parable however is not concerned with such things either. Its background is something completely different.

The Israelites were convinced that riches were a sign of divine favor and poverty a proof of desertion by God. The sadducees did not believe at all in a life after death. And for the others the next world was only a shadowy kingdom. So whoever served God must receive his reward already in this life. "That it may go well with thee and thou mayest live long upon the earth." It is against this materialistic earthly outlook that Christ directs his parable. And it is for this reason that he paints the contrast in the harshest colors. The rich man lives in incredible luxury, the poor in indescribable misery. Accordingly the first must surely be blessed by God, the second accursed.

Then the curtain falls and the second act in the next world shows us the opposite. The rich man was one deserted by God and the poor a beloved of the lord. And so it goes badly for the first in the next world and well for the second. Abraham says to the reveler: "Everything went well for you during your life, but for Lazarus on the other hand things went badly. Now he is here consoled but you are tortured" (6:25). Material well being is thus in no way synonymous with happiness. Earthly poverty is likewise not the same as misfortune. The Jewish standard is false. But materialism has so corroded the thinking not only of the Jews but of all men that Christ says in the parable that even someone returning from the dead to inform them would accomplish nothing. So it was then. So it is today. Over and over again men confuse riches with happiness and poverty with misfortune. But the judgment of God is completely different. It is not determined by the material. Death can bring about a complete revolution and make the blessed miserable and the miserable blessed. Those who in this world stand on the uppermost branch of well being can, in certain circumstances, be bottommost in the next, and vice versa. Financial income and the size of the bank account are in no way proportional to the grace of God. For a century and a half now through marxism the economic has been represented as the only determining factor, and with it has come an overstressing of the commercial. At the same time the Manchester school of false liberalism loosed an unrestrained economic war. Thus the material standard of living and economic well being has moved so much to the center in both the life of the individual and the thought of the classes and nations that mammon has actually become the idol of this century. Whoever is not primarily concerned about his financial advancement is considered either lazy or an unrealistic fanatic. And on the other hand anyone who does attain well being and riches is commonly thought to have mastered life and forged his fortune.

And yet one has come back from the dead, Jesus Christ himself, and has said to them that they must reexamine their values because the standard of God does not coincide with theirs, and because earthly material happiness can lead to eternal unhappiness, as earthly unhappiness can lead to eternal happiness. But he preaches to deaf ears. They know better. Only when the second act on the other side of the iron curtain of humanity begins will their eyes be opened. But then it is too late. Their chase after fortune has then ended with the plunge into misfortune. And then the unfortunate for whom one had here only a sympathetic shrug of the shoulders will find happiness. The new christian teaching is a difficult matter. The shrieking colors of the parable, the startling contrast between the reveler and Lazarus leave absolutely nothing to be desired for clarity. Anyone seeking a false happiness now has no excuse.

OF ARCHITECTS AND GENERALS

Lk 14:25-33: "If anyone comes to follow me and does not hate his father and mother, his wife and children, his brothers and sisters, and even his life, he cannot be my disciple. He who comes to follow me but will not shoulder his cross cannot be my disciple. Really, which of you, intending to build a tower, will not first sit down and calculate the cost, to see whether he has the wherewithal to finish it? Otherwise, if after laying a foundation he has not money enough to complete the work, the curious crowd will indulge in mockery at his expense. 'Here is a fellow,' they will say, 'who began building without having means enough to finish!' Or, again, where is there a king that intends to mobilize his troops against a rival king, but does not first sit down and hold a council to see whether he with his ten thousand men is a match for the other who mobilizes twenty thousand to attack him? And if he is not, he sends an embassy to inquire about terms of peace while the other is still far off. On the same principle, none of you can be my disciple unless he first renounces all his possessions."

For building one needs money, and for waging war soldiers. He who begins to build without financial reserves will have to desert the uncompleted work after a short time or incur debts from which he will not emerge for the rest of his life, or declare himself bankrupt. He who goes to war without the necessary military forces will have to pay with his honor or even his freedom and his life. It has always been this way. When Christ compares his stipulations to his followers with the money of the architect and the soldiers of the general, he gives the parable an extremely remarkable turn. It is to be expected that for the complete dedication to Christ one must, like the architect and general, possess something. But Christ inverts the demand: for the complete imitation of Christ there is needed not a possession but a renunciation. The kingdom of God follows other laws than the undertakings of men. In these it is natural power and means that are needed. In the kingdom of God the complete renunciation of one's own strength is required for the strength of God to develop completely. Complete dedication to Christ certainly does not refer to the usual human life now extended to include Christ, the usual human construction to which a special story is now attached, the usual human battle for which new goals are valid. It means something completely different. It is an action of God which man must not obstruct, but rather clear the way for and to which he yields and submits completely.

It means renunciation of external possessions, and indeed, as Christ expressly says, "all possessions." Man must have his hands free, may not drag ballast along. He may not, through attachment to house and home, to furniture and money, become too ponderous and immovable. In his imitation of Christ he must also lead the counterattack against materialism; he must lead a mammon-free life in order to overcome the service of mammon; he must throw all weight on the side of poverty in order to bring the scales of humanity, which so often are drawn down on the side of the material, into some measure of equilibrium.

He must also sacrifice human attachments: "Father and mother, wife and child, brother and sister." He must, as Jesus had already as a 12 year old boy formulated it in the temple, "be about his father's business." He can therefore not make himself comfortable in a bourgeois Nazareth.

Finally the imitation of Christ demands a renunciation of one's own ego. And this too is complete renunciation. One must give "his own life."

The battle against human egoism, against selfishness asserting itself in all places and at all times, is exacted through the resignation of self-centeredness, through self-denial. Thus in the imitation of Christ it is not a matter of carrying out his ideas and plans oneself but of renouncing all in order to be only a tool in the hands of another, only a messenger who is in the employ of another. It is a complete merging in the flowing river of Christ. The only thing that man can and should retain is—according to the express formulation of Jesus—the cross. "Whoever does not bear his cross and follow me cannot be my disciple." The only possession is the sign of sacrifice, the surrender to death. Christ summons the men who will enter fully into his service, completely and exclusively. With the jealousy of God, of which the bible often speaks, he sees that man belongs to no one else but him.

It is an unheard of, a radical demand, a total claim, a challenge to unresting effort and unconditional surrender. Christ formulates this parable for those who in the first overflow of enthusiasm offer their surrender without ripened serious consideration. Christ is showing them the entire burden, the deep seriousness and the final consequence of their consent. Rather not build than have to stop in the middle of the building. Rather confer immediately with an opponent than take the chance. Rather not resolve upon exclusive service to Christ than go only half way. Half way is half renunciation. But anyone who retains a few things, who encloses a few stipulations and conditions, who builds somewhere a last retreat of security in order not to deliver himself over completely and unconditionally to the lord, he has entered upon the imitation of Christ unconsidered. Complete surrender means to demolish the bridges behind one, to burn the ships.

Anyone who believes that he has been called must test himself to see whether he is prepared to fulfill these conditions, as the architect must examine his finances and undertake an estimate, and the commander-in-chief count his troops and test their striking force. Enthusiasm alone does not suffice. The sign of authenticity is preparedness for complete denial. The final enormity and the deep seriousness of the challenge of Christ are here visible. There is only one who nevertheless induces men to dare this step, smilingly to shove everything to the side and to speak the unconditional affirmation. This one is Christ the lord, before whose greatness everything else shrinks and disappears, before whose splendor all earthly light pales, before whose love all human love fades. Therefore Christ begins his exorbitant demand with the simple and yet lucid words: "If someone will come to me." It is denial for the sake of complete gain, poverty for the sake of great riches, loneliness for the sake of the most joyous company, renunciation of the ego for the glorification of the alone great thou. In short it is the giving up of everything for the sake of surrender to Christ.

Sin

THE LOST SON

Lk 15:11–31: "Once upon a time a man had two sons. One day the younger of them said to his father: 'Father, give me the part of the property that falls to my share.' So he divided his property between them. Not many days later, the younger son cashed everything and went off to a far-off country, where he squandered his money by licentious living. When he had spent everything, a terrible famine swept over that country and he faced starvation. So he went to throw himself on the mercy of a citizen of that region, who sent him to his barn to tend pigs. And oh, how heartily he would have feasted on the pods on which the pigs were feeding! But no one would give them to him. At last he came to his senses. 'How many of my father's hired men,' he said, 'have food enough and to spare, while I am here perishing with hunger! I will quit this place and go to meet my father. Father, I will say to him, I have sinned against heaven, and you know that I am no longer fit to be considered your son. Treat me as one of your hired help.' So he quit the place and went to meet his father.

"He was still a good way off when his father caught sight of him and, stirred to pity, ran and threw his arms round his neck and kissed him affectionately.

119

"The son then said to him: 'Father, I have sinned against heaven and before you, and you know that I am no longer fit to be considered your son.' But the father said to his slaves: 'Quick; bring out the finest robe and put it on him; then put a ring on his hand and sandals on his feet; also get the fatted calf and kill it; let us feast and celebrate. This son of mine was dead and has come back to life again, was lost and has been found again.' And so they gave themselves up to celebrating.

"Meanwhile the elder son was in the field. When he returned and came near the house, he heard strains of music and dancing, and, calling one of the farmhands aside, inquired what all this meant. 'Why,' the lad said to him, 'your brother has come back; so your father had the fatted calf killed because he received him back safe and sound.' Therefore he grew angry and refused to go in. So his father came out and pleaded with him. But he protested and said to the father: 'Look at all these years that I have been toiling like a slave for you! I never disobeyed any of your orders, and yet you never gave me a kid, that I might celebrate with my friends! But here comes that son of yours who wasted his property in the company of lewd women, and right away you kill the fatted calf to humor him!' He replied: 'My son, you have always been with me, and all that is mine is yours; but as to this feasting and celebrating— it simply has to be done, because that brother of yours was dead and has come to life again, was lost and has been found again!' "

The first figure: the younger son is denied the right of primogeniture. So he can make no career at home on the estate. Aside from that he was convinced that he had already long outgrown children's ways and was no longer to be led around docilely. A real man should be his own forger of his fortune. And above all one must have seen the world. So he had his portion paid to him and went out into the wide world full of plans and hopes. A young man with breeding and money need not wait long for a feminine following. But this innocent country boy did not once notice what kind of riff-raff was buzzing around him. After they had completely pumped him dry they threw him away like a sucked out egg. And now things deteriorate rapidly until he lands with the swine. It was not only socially the lowest step, but for a Jew also religiously polluting. Anyone working with a charitable group or in a social institution knows that often enough not only the way to love but also the way to conversion is through the stomach. "Many of my father's hired men have food to spare, and I perish of hunger." Finally the enforced loneliness led the young man to inner insight and conversion. So he picks up courage and returns. It is a real conversion of 180 degrees. Haughty, rich and self-confident he had left. Humiliated, ragged and wretched he returns.

This symbolic picture of heathendom sketched by Christ is shocking. Humanity has wasted and squandered on the way the spiritual, moral, religious inheritance that God gave it. The false self-confidence, the autocratic conduct has led to catastrophe. God is deserted and the idols of mammon, of sexuality and of the feeling of power are set up in his place. The defection from God and the worship of idols is, according to the bible, always a throwing away of oneself on whores and harlots. And the whole thing ends not only in material and economic need, in self-incurred misery, but in filth. A secularized world which has deserted and lost the authority of God, the home of the kingdom of God, the riches of God's grace arrives out of inner necessity at the dead end of unbelief. There one can either confirm oneself in sullen stubbornness or with false heroism dramatize oneself in the attitude of despair. Or one may draw the logical consequences from his insight and find his way back to faith and to a newly acquired happiness, now valued in a different way and in the future better defended. The parable is like a history of humanity in the past one hundred and fifty years.

The second figure: the father waits. There are two aspects to be considered here. First, the fact that he neither restrains the runaway son nor goes after him. The son must experience with his own body what things are like outside. The man who wishes no grace should feel what life without grace is and recognize that he is designated for grace and mercy if he does not wish to degenerate in body and soul. God waits. He waits for the wanderings of single men and for the misdirected journeyings of entire peoples. He has created man for freedom and therefore does not restrain him even from deciding falsely within this freedom. God knows that the converted are often truer than men who have never fallen. The way through sin is a way to appreciation of grace. And the temporary falling away from God can lead to greater glorification of God. Even sin can be a way to God.

There is a second aspect to this waiting. The father of this parable has not given up his son, still less condemned him. He waits silently. He believes in the good that lies in this young man, hopes that the glimmering wick will again light up and loves even the lost. God also waits with peoples, generations and with entire humanity. It is never too late for an insight. No situation is hopeless. There would be a basis for pessimism only if God did not wait. Every conversion finds open arms. Not even the full confession of wretchedness of the one returning is conceded. For all is overshadowed in the ceremonious joy of the return home, in dance, music, fine dress and celebration. The broken reed becomes a blossoming tree. There is not a word of a severe sermon, no hint of philippics, no pedantic "I told you so," no moralizing "That's what happens." But a greater love and a closer tie come as a result of the meeting anew of the father and son.

The third figure: the firstborn, favored from the beginning, presents a deplorable picture. One gets the impression that he remained at home not at all out of the greatness of his character but out of a lack of temperament and out of bourgeois convention. He lacks any nobility. He is unhappy to see the return home of the wayward. Angry and pouting he stands aloof. He counts up his own merits, laments that he is not sufficiently appreciated, is not really aware of the security he enjoys in the house of his father and leads a dull life of respectability. Christ wishes to sketch Israel, the chosen, favored people of God, who in pharisaical complacency imagine themselves better than others, extol their own accomplishments and are not at all inclined to open the gate of the kingdom of heaven to anyone else. It is however also a sign of a false piety which is to be found not only in the Israel of that time but also in the christianity of today. Every imagining oneself better than others, every sulky tarrying in the musty corners of exclusiveness, criticizing the Godless outside, every passing of impatient hard-hearted judgments, every secret desire that God's lightning annihilate all the Godless, is here shown as unspiritual, contradicting the waiting, universal, magnanimous, tireless spirit of God.

The situation of the lost son is extremely contemporary. There is no lack of those who wish to rise up in order to return. But unfortunately there is also no lack of others who, frowning, find that they are not sufficiently recompensed for their model bearing, and who do not approve God's being prepared to distribute his grace with full hands to those who have shown themselves unworthy. Let us hope that the solemn feast of ecclesiastical joy will burst all doors and attract the motley masses of the wayward.

THE GOOD SHEPHERD

Lk 15:3–7: "Suppose one of you has a hundred sheep: will he not, if he lose one of them, leave the ninety-nine in the desert and go in search of the one that is lost until he finds it? And when he has found it, he joyfully puts it on his shoulders, and, on coming home, calls his friends and neighbors together and says to them: 'Congratulate me, for I have found my sheep that was lost.' I tell you, there is joy in heaven over one repentant sinner—more, in fact, than over ninety-nine saints that have no need of repentance."

Jesus' attitude is a surprise. Nothing contradicts the holy God more than sin and sinners. Nothing lies closer to him than holiness and the holy or, as the old testament would say, righteousness and the righteous. It is therefore to be expected that Jesus, the incarnate God, would place himself in the holy city Jerusalem at the side of the priests serving in the temple and the pharisees officially designated as righteous. But the opposite is the case. He "eats with tax collectors and sinners," associates with them by preference and seeks them out. He explains his reasons in the parable of the shepherd who leaves his ninety-nine sheep in order to seek the one lost, for in heaven there is more joy over one sinner who is converted than over ninety-nine who need no conversion.

In this parable we find above all *consolation:* we all belong to the lost. We time and again lose our way spiritually, let God

124

drop from sight and occupy ourselves with a thousand other things rather than with God's word and God's will. We have erred in our hearts, for our love belongs often enough to things and men who contradict God. Above all we have erred in our lives, for the sincere man knows that he is a sinner. Return is not possible of our own strength, and so we are like the sheep which has run away from the herd and lies helplessly with a broken leg in some hole, completely dependent on the arrival and help of the good shepherd. It is specifically this arrival and help that is described in the parable. "When he has found his sheep, he lifts it joyfully to his shoulders. And when he comes home, he calls his friends and neighbors together and says to them: Rejoice with me, for I have found my sheep that was lost." So we know that Christ seeks us out even if we wander on false paths, that he bears us back with the strength of grace where our own strength fails, that he rejoices over our conversions, which are indeed his doing. So too sin can glorify God if it leads to conversion. And the sinner who finds his home through God's grace does not lead an inferior existence and a Cinderella life in the kingdom of God, but he is the cause of genuine and honest joy in the entire kingdom of God.

On the other hand the parable is a *warning* to all who are in the service of the church. To conserve does not suffice. The demand is to missionize. The church is not an institution for the bettering of the good; it exists for the rescuing of the lost. All of us bear a part of the responsibility for these lost. The mission must not be forgotten and the dynamics must not be left to rust. Among these lost are the unbelieving, whether they are old or new pagans. To the lost belong the great working masses. The church seeks them out with special pastoral care for workers,

workers' organizations and its many social foundations. But the lost also include many educated people. In preaching one must be guided by the average, and so take little notice of the questions and difficulties which directly imperil the faith of the educated. For them too special pastoral care is necessary. To preserve catholicism among catholic peoples and in catholic countries the missionizing must move directly into the diaspora. The church has expressly changed its canon law in order to meet this task with its secular institutes, which pursue the lost.

Fulfillment of the Kingdom of God

Reform

THE WEEDS IN THE FIELD

Mt 13:24–30: "The kingdom of heaven reminds me of a man who has sown good seed in his field. But, while everybody is asleep, an enemy comes and sows weeds among the wheat, and goes away. Eventually the blades spring up and put forth heads, but by that time the weeds also crop out. So the help of the landowner approach him and say: 'Sir, was it not good seed that you sowed in your field? How, then, is it overrun with weeds?' 'That is the work of an enemy!' he replies. 'Well,' say the help to him, 'do you want us to go and gather them up?' 'Not at all,' he answers; 'otherwise, in gathering the weeds, you might pull up the wheat along with them. Let both grow until the harvest, and, when harvest time has come, I will say to the reapers: 'Gather up, first of all, the weeds and bind them in bundles to be burnt; after that, store the wheat in my barn.' "

Mt 13:37–43: "The sower of the good seed is the Son of Man. The field is the world. The good seed are the born citizens of the realm. The weeds are the brood of the wicked one. The enemy who planted them is the devil. The harvest time is the end of the world. The reapers are the angels. Just as the weeds, therefore, are gathered in bundles and burnt, so it will be at the end of the world: the Son of Man will send his angels, and they will weed his kingdom of all seducers and evildoers, and hurl them into the fiery furnace. There it is that weeping and gnashing of teeth will really be heard. Then the saints will shine like the sun in the kingdom of their Father. Let everyone heed what he has heard."

127

We face a painful fact. The church should be the great sign of God, the lasting miracle which again and again amid world events points to the mysterious strength of God. It must be the question mark that no one can overlook, an elevated banner, the fluttering flag of God. It must be apparent that all the gates of this church stand open and that men and people uninterruptedly file in. Like Michael it must as an angel of the lord fight the battles of God with the sword of the spirit. In its popes one must see the awe-inspiring form of Christ, in its bishops one must feel the spirit of the apostles. One should see in the lives of its priests that in their hands the miracle of the multiplication of the loaves takes place. And the faithful must all have the shining eyes which are the mirror of a pure heart and of inner peace. All then would be immersed in the atmosphere of love; a singularly happy and bold step would be taken toward light. Such a church would be irresistible. It would draw all eyes to itself, captivate all spirits and conquer all hearts. The First Vatican Council in the last century still had the courage to write the audacious statement: "The Church is of herself an uncontradictable witness of her divine mission through her amazing propagation, towering holiness, inexhaustible fruitfulness in all good works, her comprehensive unity and unconquerable steadfastness. Thus she is a sign erected among the nations."

But the truth seems completely different. How many moral mortgages of history weigh upon this papacy! How much timidity and pettiness there is in the wearers of the mitre. How much of the all too human in the priests in their sanctuaries! And are believing men then really different from the unbelieving? Can one really recognize the tree of Christ by its fruits? How much kitsch there is in the houses of God in this church!

128

How much false sentimentality in her devotions! How much exaggerated formulation in her prayers! How much of the ungenuine in her piety! How much false activism and egoism in her organizations! How much anxious building of ghettos or false conformity to the world! Where is the simple grandeur of the gospel? Where is the world conquering daring of the pauline spirit? Where is the restrained ardor of the johannine mysticism?

An abyss yawns between the ideal and the real. And so for many the church is no longer the magnet which draws them but the scandal which repels them. They are amenable to the gospel but not to the church. They can affirm the articles of the faith of catholicism but they cannot come to terms with the reality of the concrete church. Many turn away in painful disappointment. They are become poorer in losing a great hope. For others the towering city of God has remained a medieval small town which in any case one still studies out of historical interest and which still preserves its romantic aura. In the best there smoulders the passion of a Savonarola. They secretly clench their fists and wait for the reformer. Of course they do not exactly wish for the fury of Luther, which like an avalanche dragged all into the deep. They do not wish for a reformation which deserts the house abruptly, for too many heirlooms from the ancestral home are stuffed into it. But they wish for a reform. Nothing is helped by a few little decrees. They wish with real radicalism to attack the whole. The church is, according to the words of the apostle Paul, the mystical body of Christ. But because Christ is the God-man there may and should also be the human alongside the divine in the church. They are amenable therefore to human words, methods and forms throughout. But in Christ there is nothing of the only too human narrowness, pettiness, hatefulness and sin. How can there be human weaknesses in the mystical body of the lord? This is the salient point. Herein lies the real scandal. Here the lever of reform must be applied. This all too human must be eradicated root and branch. So they argue.

And do they not deserve our full sympathy? Just like that servant who has tilled a field with great effort and sowed the wheat and who now sees to his distressed and painful surprise a crowd of weeds growing and in the fury of his radicalism suggests tearing out all the weeds immediately. But the amazing answer of Christ is like a stream of cold water on the reformers' fire. "Let it grow!" The time of our earthly life is a time of trial. And precisely this trial is the real life task of man. Here on earth good and evil are not very neatly divided and separated from one another, nor should they be. Man is exposed like the wheat among the weeds. Christian life is a life amid danger, amid debate, amid contradiction and opposition. It is not world and church alongside one another, it is the church amid the world. It is belief amid unbelief. It is christian among heathen. Of course the earth is God's field. But God leaves satan to sow his diabolical weeds in the divine fields while humans sleep. To root out the evil once and for all with complete radicalism contradicts God's world plan. It would be to usurp the justice of God and in a certain measure to play God. Whoever wishes a church without human weaknesses, an angelic church with angelic priests, angelic bishops and an angelic pope thinks he knows better than Christ, the founder of the church. He wishes heaven on earth. He wishes an earthly paradise. He wishes to have in time what according to God's will is saved for eternity. There is lacking in him that spiritual magnitude and intellectual breadth which is demanded by Christ, who stresses that God lets his sun shine upon sinners and righteous, and who gives his fructifying blessing to scoundrels and saints. There is lacking in him that ability to wait which God demands. He wishes to anticipate the result without having to undergo the trial. He wishes to stand already on the mountain peak without testing to see who will persevere in the steep climb and who stay behind. He wishes to have eternity and yet does not know the meaning of time. He wishes to have men sorted out without first leaving them the possibility for decision. In short he wishes the kingdom of God, but not as Christ has wished it. It is human jingoism under a christian mask, human fanaticism under the appearance of christian zeal. The spirit of iconoclastic fanaticism, of destructive radicalism, is not the spirit of Christ. The young zealots who wish to fetch fire from heaven are rebuked by the lord: "You do not know of which spirit you are children."

Should one therefore be satisfied with everything? Put the brakes on all reform endeavors? Choke all ardor in embryo? By no means! But there is an essential difference between christian reform efforts and unchristian fanaticism. One must call the wheat wheat and the weeds weeds, must give man an eye and a sense for the genuine, for the christian, through a real spirit of faith, and at the same time be able to recognize the ungenuine, the unchristian, that which contradicts faith. One must promote the good, fight the evil, work for God and against satan, must summon men to decision and help them to decide correctly. But one must not believe that the wicked can simply be eradicated and exterminated, but rather leave this bundling and burning for the last day. For the rectification of all things comes only from the court of the lord. A little field, even if it

131

is the most pious sect and the most ideal assembly and a group of the holiest people, is never the field of God. For within it, according to the clear word of the lord, there are also weeds. The all too human in the church is therefore something which Christ expressly and consciously permits. This must not be an offense and a scandal to us but only an occasion to see things correctly in faith and to decide things correctly through faith. The church of Christ is in this time and in this world and therefore is also burdened with human weaknesses. The statement of Vatican I is accurate: the church's fruitfulness, unity, steadfastness are not to be explained on a purely natural level and are therefore a sign of God. But the essence of this church is accessible only to faith, because alongside all the great and divine the small, human and even all too human also adheres to this church. He who sees the field of the lord full of wheat and weeds should remember the parable of the lord about the wheat and weeds and recognize this very field as the field of Christ.

Watchfulness

THE PARABLE OF THE LORD AND THE SERVANTS

Lk 12:36–48: " 'Be like men who are on the lookout for their master, uncertain when he starts for home from the wedding feast. Thus, the moment he arrives, they will at once open the door for him. Well for those slaves whom the master on his return finds awake. I assure you, he will gird himself and bid them recline at table and personally wait on them! And whether he returns before midnight or after, well for those slaves if he finds them so engaged! Of one thing you are sure: if the owner of a house knew at what hour the thief was coming, he would stay awake and not let his house be broken into. So you, too: be in constant readiness; the Son of Man returns at an hour you do not expect.'

"Here Peter interposed: 'Lord, do you mean your parable for us or for everybody else as well?' The Lord replied: 'Suppose a master puts a manager in charge of his household to distribute the rations of food at the proper time—in that case, who is the faithful, prudent manager? It is the slave whom the master on his return finds attending to his duties; and a happy man is he! I tell you truly, he will put him in charge of his entire estate. But if the manager says to himself: "My master is long in coming," and then proceeds to maltreat the men and women slaves, and to eat and to drink till he is drunk, the master of that overseer will return on a day he is not expecting him and at an hour not known to him, and shall separate him, and assign him a place among the unbelievers.

" 'If such an overseer knows his master's intention, yet fails to make preparations or act according to his intentions, he will be severely punished. Of course, if he does not know them, yet does things that deserve punishment, he will be but slightly punished. Anyone that has received much will be required to return much; and he that has a large capital entrusted to him will be required to pay back interest as well.' "

Still another parable of the end of time is added by the lord. This parable is based on oriental life of that time. The master of the house is invited to a banquet. His slaves remain at home, knowing that the lord will return late at night. But the exact time of his return he has not told them. The conduct of the individuals now varies radically.

One is negligent. Another lets himself go. He misuses the other servants and maids, sets to work in the cellar and kitchen and has for himself a wild mad evening until he is dead drunk. But other servants stay up to see that the lamps remain lit so that the master can come into a well lighted house. They stand in their uniforms prepared to carry out his instructions. One especially distinguishes himself.

Unexpectedly the lord returns early. The first, negligent servant receives his thrashing. The second is executed. What happens to the watchful servants is unthinkable by human standards: the lord invites the slaves to table and serves them himself. And he who had excelled is named administrator of all the property of the lord.

The temporal and the eschatalogical are mixed together in this parable. The return of the lord is the second coming of Christ in judgment. Whoever has done evil will be punished. Whoever has lived dissolutely gets "his place among the unbelievers," that is, he is excluded from the kingdom of God. Those prepared and waiting are invited to the heavenly banquet. The servants have become friends, the slaves the chosen. They are members of the household of God.

The parable demands a spirit of watchful preparedness and true stewardship over that which God has committed to man. Life is a commission. The conduct in this world determines the next world. The degree of temporal preparedness earns corresponding payment or punishment in eternity.

But this is payment only in a transferred sense. For the payment is itself a grace. In order to make this point clear Christ seizes upon just this image of the servant. "Suppose some one of you has a slave who is plowing or tending sheep, and then comes in from the field. Will he say to him: 'Come here at once and recline at table'? Will he not, rather, say to him: 'Get my dinner ready; and gird yourself to wait on me while I eat and drink; after that, you can eat and drink'? Does he feel obliged to the slave for carrying out his orders? Apply this to yourselves:

when you have carried out all the orders given you, just say: 'We are good-for-nothing slaves; we have merely done our duty'" (Lk 17:7–10). In the first parable Jesus says that the master of the house serves the servants. In the second he stresses that he has himself served by the servants. The apparent contradiction should now make clear that it is purely and freely a grace of God when he, besides making demands of men, also gives to them. As creation, and doubly as sinful creation, man has no claims at all upon God. When God in this case repays the actions of men it is not payment on the basis of work which includes a legal title, rather it is recompense on the basis of the will and the promise of God, who so attaches his grace to the work that what is a free gift appears as a recompense.

Preparedness

THE PARABLE OF THE WISE AND FOOLISH MAIDENS

Mt 25:1–13: "On that day the same will happen in the kingdom of heaven that once happened to ten bridesmaids who, being provided with their lamps, had gone out to meet the bridegroom. Now, five of these were foolish, and five wise: the foolish, though provided with their lamps, had yet taken no oil with them; the wise, on the contrary, had besides their lamps taken oil with them in their jars. But the bridegroom was long in coming, and so they all nodded off to slumber and, finally, slept. Suddenly, at midnight, a shout is raised: 'Wake up there! The bridegroom! Come out to meet him!' At this, all the bridesmaids woke up and began to trim their lamps. Then the foolish said to the wise: 'Give us some of your oil; our lamps are going out.' But the wise demurred. 'There might not be oil enough both for us and for you,' they said; 'better go to the dealers and buy some for yourselves.' So they went to buy some; but meanwhile the bridegroom arrived, and those who were ready entered with him to take part in the festivities. Then the door was barred. Later the other bridesmaids arrived; but when they pleaded, 'Sir, sir, open the door for us,' back came his answer, 'Upon my word, I have nothing to do with you.' Keep awake therefore; you know neither the day nor the hour."

The unbearable heat is finally relieved through the evening coolness. The bridegroom with his friends sets out for the neighboring village to fetch his bride. She has passed the last days of her freedom with her girlfriends, and now they wait until the wedding procession comes. It drags on, and because the celebration will last on into the morning the maidens take some sleep in advance. About midnight they suddenly start up. The joyful shouts of the young men can be heard in the street, and so the lights must be quickly lit. It appears then that a few of the maidens, who have of course brought their lamps along, have forgotten their oil supply. The answer of those who have not forgotten sounds very unchristian. They refuse to share, and take care only of themselves. Then the procession returns to the other village. The feasting and dancing begin. It is of course understandable why the carefully barricaded door to the festive house is not opened to the late stragglers who have procured some oil through a second hand dealer, for all kinds of rabble are idling about outside. Nevertheless the answer of the bridge-groom also sounds unchristian. He refuses to open and treats those knocking outside like unknown strangers.

But this parable is not concerned with understanding, sharing and sympathy; rather it is a *parable of man's final end*. And when the end has come, in death for individuals, on the day of judgment for humanity, then there is no more time, for time itself has come to an end. One is then either prepared and equipped or one is not. What was neglected can then no more be retrieved. There is no longer time to compensate for what is lacking. Therefore the charge states: be watchful and prepared.

This holds for individuals. It is dangerous to push off preparedness until the life to come. For perhaps later there will be no more time to set things right. Man can die suddenly through a heart attack, be killed in an accident, fall a victim to a bombardment in war. And even if he passes sick days on his deathbed he will perhaps no longer have the spiritual strength to change his attitude, to collect himself, to pray. He needs his entire strength to bear his illness and to lead the physical fight against suffocating death. And it is unworthy of God to postpone readiness for his call until old age, to dedicate merely the wretched remainder of one's life to him. Whether he will then still give the grace is questionable. Therefore preparedness is necessary in life, in the fullness and on the pinnacle of life. In another parable the lord says expressly that death comes like a thief in the night, unexpectedly, unanticipated. Whoever is not prepared is lost.

This warning also holds true for humanity. We do not know how long world history will continue before the end of the world will break in. The astronomical catastrophe through which our sun-splinter earth will run into destruction can instantly set upon us. In the meanwhile men and peoples act as if they still had thousands of years securely before them. Hardly anyone thinks seriously of the possibility of a sudden end of the world. What was still obvious to the primitive church, the waiting for the second coming of the lord, has become something distantly and completely foreign to our christianity of today. One clasps

137

himself to the earth and to this life, still plans on tremendous possibilities of progress and loses his view of the end, loses his eschatological attitude which is demanded so urgently by the bible. In the parable Christ speaks of five wise and five foolish maidens. It is questionable whether the proportion would still be so favorable today, or whether one would have have to increase the number of the foolish substantially. To which do we belong?

Christ as Fulfillment

CHRIST AS THE SHEPHERD OF THE PEOPLES

Jn 10:1–16: " 'I tell you the plain truth: he who does not enter the sheepfold by the door, but climbs into it some other way, is a thief and a robber. But he who enters by the door is the shepherd of the sheep. He is the one for whom the keeper opens the door; and the sheep hear his voice. He calls his own sheep individually, and leads them out. After taking out all that are his own, he marches in front of them; and the sheep follow him because they know his voice. But they will never follow a stranger; on the contrary, they run away from him, because they do not know the voice of strangers.' This was the parable Jesus told them; but they did not grasp the meaning of what he said to them.

"Jesus resumed, therefore. 'I must be very plain with you,' he said to them; 'I am the door for the sheep; any and all that came before me are thieves and robbers. But the sheep did not listen to them. I am the door; if one goes in through me, all will be well with him; he will go in and out, and find pasture. The thief does not come except to steal and slaughter and destroy. I have come that they may have life and have it in abundance.

" 'I am the good shepherd. A good shepherd lays down his life to save his sheep. If a hired man, who is not a shepherd and has no sheep of his own, sees the wolf coming, he abandons the sheep and runs away; and the wolf carries them off or scatters them. After all, he is only a hired man and has no interest in the sheep. I am the good shepherd; and I know mine and mine know me, as the Father knows me and I know the Father; and I lay down my life to save the sheep. Still other sheep I claim as my own, which are not of this fold. I must lead them also to pasture, and they will listen to my voice, and there will be one flock, one shepherd.' "

The Israelites were in their early period a nation of shepherds. Therefore the image of the leader of the people as a shepherd of her herds was familiar and current to them. Moses had received his call as he drove his herds toward Mount Horeb. He was to be the shepherd of the people of God. David is anointed and taken away from the herd to be king over Israel. Over and over the prophets use the image of the shepherd and their eager or sluggish care for the herds. Jesus is completely rooted in the tradition of his people. And so this image is also familiar to him. That the metaphor occurs several times among his parables and in several variations is therefore understandable. According to his teaching it is the inner attitude, the intention of the shepherd that is the decisive factor. The hireling is paid. In the hour of danger he seeks only to save his own skin, for in his contract nowhere is the duty of risking his life during an emergency mentioned.

The charge holds first of all for the spiritual leaders of the people, whose name of pastor even today recalls the simile of the shepherd. When a priest is only a paid office holder, considers his profession only a means of livelihood and a bread basket, reduces his activity as a consequence to a minimum and in times of danger immediately looks out for his own welfare, he is a hireling who wears priestly robes dishonestly. But one may not think merely of the external dangers of life. The priest as shepherd must become personally involved in his work and he may not yield even if the opposition takes away his good name, speaks slanderously of him and deals unfairly with him in all ways. He stays at his post and stands up to the demands of God and his own conscience, even if as a result he is labeled a backwoodsman and his inflexibility condemned as narrow-minded obstinacy. This personal involvement of course must not mean trying to run other people's lives.

The parable however is valid also for the *worldly leaders* of the people. Government men who consider their offices only as well paying posts, officers who lead their command only for the satisfaction of their ambitions, professors and teachers who look only for good pay and are happy when the schoolday is at an end and their own lives begin, writers and journalists who are not conscious of the responsibility they bear for the spiritual and moral welfare of the public and the nation, are all without exception hirelings. When the man must expose himself, when his person forms the target for criticism, when his interpretations contradict public opinion, then begins the hour of trial in which the genuine is separated from the false, the hireling distinguished from the good shepherd. The issue is not decided by stipends and royalties, not by position and titles, but by the will and readiness to undertake responsibility, to be there for the sake of others, to consider their welfare as a life task. All professions abound today with hirelings. The real shepherds are only seldom found. Therefore the flocks are easily penetrated by the communistic bears and the nihilistic wolves, doubly easily when these people understand how to use the demonic art of camouflage to clothe themselves in the sheep's clothing of harmlessness, of the public good.

This parable of the shepherd also finds its living embodiment in Christ. He himself stresses this fact with the words: "I am the good shepherd." There are three aspects to this truth.

The first is the *knowledge of his own*. "I know mine and mine know me." There is an exchange relationship of knowledge, and yet how different is this knowledge! Christ knows his own better than they know themselves. He knows the weak and their refusals, their meanness and pettiness, but also their good will and their longing for improvement and growth. His own know him but indeed never know him entirely. For he bursts all human frames, he is essentially the inconceivable and incomprehensible; and yet a knowledge of him is given to men of faith through that peculiar exchange relationship. That call and answer, that speaking and listening, that attraction and love are possible only in the imitation of Christ.

The second inference that Jesus draws is the *leading of his own*. He leads them to good pasture. Someone outside gets the opposite impression. For Christ leads his own on the steep and stony path, the bloody road that leads to Golgotha. He goes before them through dark ravines of suffering, over boulder strewn slopes of privation and toil, up steep ascents before which the masses hesitate and only the exceptional follow, over the ridge of danger to the summit of holiness. If the shepherd did not go before, the sheep would refuse to follow. But the sight of his form reaffirms the goal.

The third thing which Jesus promises is *the giving of his life in danger*. Here, like no one else, he has proved himself the good shepherd. Alone he has taken his stand against the enemy.

141

Before jewish and gentile judges he justified his actions; despite torture and torment he did not give up his task. Through suffering and blood he protected his own. In derision and ridicule he watched over the loyal and offered up his heart's blood for them. Ever since then we know that the metaphor of the good shepherd is no pastoral idyll, no sentimental blowing on rustic pipes, no picnic on a green meadow, but responsibility, care, resignation, giving up of reputation and risk of life.

So Christ is the towering form of the good shepherd, and he is shepherd not merely for a small group. His leadership is not the privilege of a few elect or a certain class or a privileged race or a chosen people. "I have other sheep who are not of this flock. I must also lead them." And he will not rest until this great uniting of peoples in the one church is achieved, until the image of *one* shepherd and *one* flock has become a reality. It is not human efforts that are decisive in the achievement of this distant goal; only Christ himself will finally bring the distant near to him and make real the great unity in him, the one. In the measure that all responsible leaders are filled with his spirit of selfless care, in the measure that all look to him, the movement toward him develops. For despite all bad experiences and all opposition we may not let the goal and the ideal out of our eyes: Christ as the one shepherd of a united people. The parable of the good shepherd has therefore a universal character.

Parables